SIR JOHN HARGRAVE'S

MISCHIEF MAKER'S MANUAL

THIS BOOK IS SO
AWESOME
IT IS ILLEGAL IN 13 STATES

DON'T GET CAUGHT

M3

EST.1909

GROSSET & DUNLAP

GROSSET & DUNLAP
Published by the Penguin Group
Penguin Group (USA) Inc., 375 Hudson Street, New York, New York 10014, USA
Penguin Group (Canada), 90 Eglinton Avenue East, Suite 700, Toronto,
Ontario M4P 2Y3, Canada
(a division of Pearson Penguin Canada Inc.)
Penguin Books Ltd., 80 Strand, London WC2R 0RL, England
Penguin Group Ireland, 25 St. Stephen's Green, Dublin 2, Ireland
(a division of Penguin Books Ltd.)
Penguin Group (Australia), 250 Camberwell Road,
Camberwell, Victoria 3124, Australia
(a division of Pearson Australia Group Pty. Ltd.)
Penguin Books India Pvt. Ltd., 11 Community Centre, Panchsheel Park,
New Delhi—110 017, India
Penguin Group (NZ), 67 Apollo Drive, Rosedale, North Shore 0632, New Zealand
(a division of Pearson New Zealand Ltd.)
Penguin Books (South Africa) (Pty.) Ltd., 24 Sturdee Avenue,
Rosebank, Johannesburg 2196, South Africa

Penguin Books Ltd., Registered Offices:
80 Strand, London WC2R 0RL, England

Text copyright © 2009 by John Hargrave. Illustrations copyright © 2009 by Grosset &
Dunlap. All rights reserved. Published by Grosset & Dunlap, a division of Penguin Young
Readers Group, 345 Hudson Street, New York, New York 10014. GROSSET & DUNLAP is a
trademark of Penguin Group (USA) Inc. Manufactured in China.

Book design by Meagan Bennett. Typeset in ITC New Baskerville and Avenir.

Library of Congress Control Number: 2008034518

ISBN 978-0-448-44982-1   10 9 8 7 6 5 4 3 2 1

Publisher's Note: All kidding aside, don't even think about trying anything in this
book before reading the Prankster's Code and Trouble. If you have one iota of
concern that a prank could harm someone's physical well-being, career, business,
reputation, or the like, don't do it. Stop, and consult a trusted adult.

SIR JOHN HARGRAVE'S

MISCHIEF MAKER'S MANUAL

THIS BOOK IS SO **AWESOME** IT IS ILLEGAL IN 13 STATES

DON'T GET CAUGHT

M3

EST. 1909

GROSSET & DUNLAP

🔺 THE BASICS

PRANK MOVES

DO-IT-YOURSELF GAGS

EXPERTS ONLY

☹ TROUBLE

🏢 ABOUT M3

WELCOME, YOUNG PRANKSTER.

You have taken the first step in your training. Congratulations.

This is a big day in your life. You're about to learn everything from proper etiquette for **Prank Phone Calls** (page 55) to usage of the classic **Smoke Bomb** (page 237). By studying the pages of *M3*, and memorizing its concepts, you'll be transformed from a novice prankster into a *mighty overlord of mayhem*. By the end of your training, you will be able to conjure forth a mighty **mountain of suds** (page 240), make **frogs rain from the sky** (page 160), and make people **fart on command** (page 143).

This manual (also known as *M3*) is the ultimate handbook for pranks, practical jokes, stunts, tricks, and large-scale hoaxes.

The best way to work through *M3* is from beginning to end. Check off each chapter as you've read it, and complete the activities for extra points. By registering at www.mischiefmakersmanual.com, you can keep track of your progress, earning awards each time you reach a new level of mischief making.

☑ After reading this introduction, you must destroy it.

THE PRANK RANKS

SECOND-CLASS MISCHIEF MAKER

FIRST-CLASS MISCHIEF MAKER

MINOR MISCHIEF MAKER

MAJOR MISCHIEF MAKER

MASSIVE MISCHIEF MAKER

MASTER MISCHIEF MAKER

THE PRANK RANKS

PRANK RANK ACHIEVED!

Congratulations, young prankster. Just for beginning your training, you have already earned the rank of **Second-Class Mischief Maker**. As you complete the sections of this book, you will earn more powerful ranks, until at last you become a Master Mischief Maker. This, young prankster, is your destiny.

☑ Visit www.mischiefmakersmanual.com to track progress and download badge.

In the first section, you will learn how to pull off **prank moves**, or simple stunts using low-cost items you probably have lying around the house. These are the building blocks of more complicated pranks, so learn them well, grasshopper.

THE BASICS

THE PERFECT PRANK

On a sleepy spring morning in 1994, the city of Boston awoke to the greatest prank the world had ever seen.

Across the Charles River from Boston there sits an enormous domed building. This famous structure belongs to the Massachusetts Institute of Technology, the greatest engineering school in the world. The building is *fifteen stories* high. Students call it "the Great Dome," both for its size and its importance. It looks like something off a dollar bill.

And on May 9, 1994, it had a police car parked on top of it.

People couldn't believe their eyes. There was no way to drive a car to the top of the huge curved building—it would be like driving a car on top of the White House. The only way to get it there would be to drop it in by helicopter, and yet no one could remember hearing a helicopter during the night. The roof of the monument was extremely difficult to access— there was an eight-foot concrete barrier encircling the dome, not to mention the hazards of wind and ice. The only way you could get up there was through a narrow trapdoor on the top.

But there it was, a police car with its lights silently flashing in the early hours of dawn. Shortly after sunrise, a crowd of onlookers began to form. The school janitors climbed to the top of the Great Dome, where they found not a police car, but a cleverly designed illusion: the outer parts of a Chevy Cavalier, attached to a wooden frame and painted to look like a campus patrol car. The pranksters' fake car looked real from the ground, but could be disassembled into smaller pieces. They pulled the pieces up the side of the dome, then reassembled them at the top. Their attention to detail was remarkable: Inside the car was a dummy dressed as a campus police officer, with a box of doughnuts at his side. Fuzzy dice hung from the rearview mirror, and the car even had a parking ticket!

Around 8:00 A.M., the local news media began to arrive, smiling and laughing at the brilliance of the prank. Because the mischief makers had left instructions for taking apart the car and getting it down from the dome safely, the maintenance crew was able to have it easily removed within a few hours. By then, Boston news stations were buzzing about the story. It made national news thanks to a reporter from the *New York Times* who wrote a funny article about it. From there, it got reported by the *Associated Press*, a worldwide news service that transmitted the story to countries as far away as India.

This, young prankster, is the pinnacle of human achievement. Forget art, history, math—those things are nice, but this is lasting. A police car on top of the Great Dome is forever.

This is what you must aspire to.

FIVE MIT DOME PRANKS

The police car wasn't the first strange object to be put on top of the Great Dome, and it won't be the last. Here are some other prank items left by MIT mischief makers:

- Working phone booth
- Fire truck
- Fake cow
- Piano
- Enormous propeller beanie

MISCHIEF, MAGNIFICENT MISCHIEF

There's ordinary mischief, and there's *magnificent* mischief. Any fool can create ordinary mischief. But only those trained in the art and science of pranking, patiently working their way through the exercises in this manual, can create *magnificent* mischief. Mischief that makes the news. Mischief that turns you into a local legend—if, indeed, you choose to reveal your

GREATEST SCHOOLS FOR PRANKING

Believe it or not, some schools "forgive and forget" when it comes to mischief, as long as students follow some variation of the **Prankster's Code** (see page 23). Ironically, the schools that are most "enlightened" about mischief are the ones your parents secretly want you to attend anyway. Make it your ambition to attend one of these exclusive, *expensive* colleges.

SCHOOL	COST	LOCATION
Massachusetts Institute of Technology (MIT)	$200,000	Cambridge, Massachusetts
California Institute of Technology (Caltech)	$160,000	Pasadena, California
Harvard University	$180,000	Cambridge, Massachusetts
Oxford University	$100,000	Oxford, United Kingdom
Stanford University	$180,000	Stanford, California

identity (many of the MIT pranksters remain anonymous to this day). Mischief that leaves your parents, your friends, and your clergyman wide-eyed with wonder.

The MIT pranksters spent two years and *hundreds of dollars* planning the stunt. Twice they tried to get the car on top of the dome, and failed. It wasn't until the *third try* that they finally got the car on the roof by developing a system of wooden rollers to make it easier to pull the pieces onto the dome.

Study this example well, young prankster, for it is a classic prank that stands as the pinnacle (so to speak) of the strange objects in strange places prank. These pranksters did everything right. They pulled this prank on the **Last Day of School** (page 68), when they would be less likely to get in trouble. And they followed a set of six guidelines known as the **Prankster's Code**, which we'll discuss in the next section.

Rather than getting in trouble for their mischief, today these pranksters are remembered as heroes, as demigods. News anchors from Boston to Bombay praised their mischief, and the school eventually put the police car on display in the MIT Museum.

Museum-quality mischief. This, young prankster, is your goal. Your training begins now.

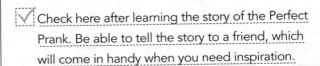

✓ Check here after learning the story of the Perfect Prank. Be able to tell the story to a friend, which will come in handy when you need inspiration.

THE PRANKSTER'S CODE

There are six fundamentals of mischief making, a set of rules that will guide and protect you throughout your pranking career. Just as a Boy Scout can stay alive in the wilderness by cooking and eating a bear, your chances of staying out of trouble will be *greatly improved* if you follow these six basic concepts.

A: Always be careful.
B: Don't be a **B**ully.
C: Be **C**reative.
D: No lasting **D**amage.
E: Excellence in pranking.
F: Be **F**unny.

A: ALWAYS BE CAREFUL

A good prank is one in which no one gets hurt—including yourself. Be smart. Use caution. Think things through. Adults will usually ignore "harmless" mischief—but the moment someone gets hurt, your pranking career is over.

Did the pranksters from the Perfect Prank run out in the middle of an ice storm, trying to lift the car to the top of the Great Dome with a stolen crane? No. They brought along extra safety ropes, emergency backup plans, and heavy-duty cabling to secure the car to the roof. When it didn't work the first two times, they stopped, went back home, and tried again later.

If you find yourself asking questions like, "What if the monkey gets loose?" or "Is smallpox really *that* dangerous?" then you've already gone too far. If you have to ask a question about someone getting hurt, then you shouldn't be doing it. End of story.

Always be careful.

B: DON'T BE A BULLY

Don't go after easy prey: younger siblings, the unpopular, the mentally handicapped. Nobody ever made the news for pranking their little brother. Prank the mayor of your town, on the other hand, and you might get on CNN.

Be *ambitious* with your mischief. In the world of pranking, "The bigger the butt cheeks, the funnier the fall."

It is important, however, to pick your targets carefully. Choose those who can take a joke, and who are not likely to retaliate by expelling you. You already know who these people are. They're the cool teachers, the laid-back parents. Everybody knows a few of these people, and they are the ripest, juiciest targets.

In the Perfect Prank, they could have put anyone's car on top of the Great Dome. They could have chosen an unpopular student (MIT has plenty of those). Instead, they used a police car.

Fight the power, not the powerless.

Don't be a bully.

C: BE CREATIVE

This manual will teach you the classic recipes for mischief, but true greatness comes from adding your own ingredients. Experiment. You should become a master chef of troublemaking, able to whip up a magnificent dish of mischief at any time.

Anything can ignite the creative spark. The MIT pranksters came up with the idea for the Perfect Prank after they found a working set of police lights at a garage sale. Someone thought, *There's got to be a use for these.* They literally built the prank around those lights.

That flash of inspiration can come from anything, even a set of flashing lights. Watch for it.

Be creative.

D: NO LASTING DAMAGE

A good prank is easily cleaned up, taken down, or thrown away. This makes it harder for anyone to press charges.

When adults get mad about mischief, they generally look for the three Ds:

- Was something Damaged?
- Was something Defaced?
- Was something Destroyed?

Your answer to all three of these questions should always be NO.

If no one was hurt (key) and nothing was damaged (also key), you've taken away their greatest weapons. To illustrate this point, the Perfect Pranksters left step-by-step instructions on how to safely remove the car from the Great Dome.

When possible, erase any evidence that you were even there. Just as a secret agent is able to get in and get out of a classified government laboratory without ever being seen, try to leave things exactly as you found them. If you encounter a locked door, for instance, you should never chop down the door with an ax, or force it open with a crowbar. Instead, you should find a creative way of getting inside the door—get a janitor to lend you a key, or see if it is unlocked at other times of day.

The prankster's rule of thumb is: **No Harm, No Foul**. This means if no serious harm occurred, no "foul" or punishment should be brought against it. This is key to staying out of trouble. If you replace someone's shampoo with raw egg (**Egghead**, page 96), they will be temporarily dripping with *egg goo*, but they can wash it off with *shampoo*, which you have thoughtfully left behind. You **did not Damage, Deface, or Destroy**. No harm, no foul.

E: EXCELLENCE IN PRANKING

The difference between *lame* mischief and *excellent* mischief is the attention to detail, the level of effort, and the pride in pulling it off. Break new ground. Don't just look for a laugh; look to become a *legend*. Lame practical jokes are for amateurs. You're a professional prankster now.

Strive for excellence.

NO HARM, NO FOWL

It's dangerous to use live animals in pranks. In 2006, a group of high school students in Maine ordered ten baby geese and forty-five chicks from a company in Indiana and set them loose inside the school. The animals covered the school with highly unsanitary **bird poo**, forcing the school to close for two days over fears of salmonella bacteria. The students were charged with criminal trespass and criminal mischief due to the damage. Their classmates hated them as well, since the two missed days were added to the end of the school year.

F: BE FUNNY

Mischief making is fun. It should also be *funny*.

The best pranks are the ones where everyone is laughing at the end—including the person who was pranked. Great pranks have the power to alter reality (for instance, a police car on a building). When they finally figure out how you did it, when reality "snaps back into place," they should laugh at your skill, planning, and mastery of the pranking craft.

Laughter is good, because it is the sign that your prank is working. The initial idea should make you laugh. While you and your partner(s) are planning, you should be laughing. You should be nervously laughing as you're pulling it off. And you should laugh for days, if not years, afterward. The longer you laugh, the better the prank was.

The Perfect Pranksters left on the police car's flashing lights, but *not the siren*. The siren would have created a disturbance, and forced the school authorities to remove the prank more quickly. The lights, on the other hand, were just **funny**.

Leave 'em laughing. They'll forgive you for just about anything.

Lame	Awesome
A **practical joke** is putting a KICK ME sign on someone's back.	A **prank** is getting a KICK ME sign onto the back of a fifty-foot statue in the middle of town.
A **practical joke** is unscrewing the caps from salt and pepper shakers.	A **prank** is switching the salt and pepper, so they shake opposite.
A **practical joke** is giving someone a wedgie.	A **prank** is proclaiming "National Wedgie Day" at the Victoria's Secret in the mall, complete with posters and flyers.

✓ Check here after memorizing the six concepts of the Prankster's Code.

HOW TO STAY OUT OF TROUBLE

The best way to stay out of trouble is to stay out of trouble.

This may seem obvious to you, but many kids *want* to get into trouble. They like the attention. These kids are idiots.

There's nothing good about trouble. Stay away from it at all costs. Do not flirt with Danger, and certainly don't ask Danger to marry you. Under no circumstances should you kiss Danger. Danger doesn't brush her teeth, and probably has rabies.

You must realize that *you are not invincible*. All mischief makers eventually find themselves in hot water (see **The Five Levels of Trouble**, page 261). That's why you must complete the following chapters: They will help you avoid *years* of potential punishment and detention time.

Learn these concepts well, young prankster, for you need a clean record to get into a good college.

THE IMPORTANCE OF APPEARANCE

Here's how you gain the trust of adults: Study hard and get good grades.

This is not a cheesy attempt to get you to behave. This is the truth. Studying hard and getting good grades provides a *smoke screen* by which adults and authority figures will not be likely to suspect you. Adults just let well-mannered kids get away with a whole lot more.

If you don't already have good grades, make a conscious effort to improve, and make sure everyone notices. Good grades are your cover.

Always try to look your best. Never swear in public. Get a haircut. Use soap. Keep your fingernails free of dirt (except, of course, when you are digging). Comb your hair. Dress respectfully. Treat adults with common courtesy.

If you don't have one already, acquire a suit (see **Looking Official**, page 41). Pullovers or cardigan sweaters are nice touches. It doesn't hurt to look like an idiot once in a while. People distrust you if you look too "slick." Strive to maintain a wholesome, Republican image. You can get away with a lot more.

CONCEAL THIS BOOK

This book can get you in trouble. Big trouble. Trouble with a capital *T*, and that rhymes with *P*, and that stands for Pranks.

Now that you have it, you must hide it. On the reverse side of the cover that fooled some adult into buying this book for you is a *plain black cover*, which is easy to camouflage by hiding it in a stack of books (see **Figure 1**).

Figure 1: *Proper removal of trick cover*

Why keep this book hidden? Because *M3* will make you guilty by association. Next time someone finds a stinking fish in a desk drawer, or a live ferret in their bed, everyone will look at you—*whether or not you even did it.* So keep quiet. Memorize the book, then eat it.

> ✓ Check here after securing a hiding place for this book. Keep the book hidden when not in use.
>
> WWW.MISCHIEFMAKERSMANUAL.COM

PLANNING

Let's say you are planning the most basic kind of mischief: **The Apple-Pie Bed** (page 76). There are still important questions to think through: How will you get access to your target's bed? What happens if someone catches you in the act? What if there's a vicious house cat hiding under the covers?

Before every prank, do your best to think through every possible thing that could go wrong. Try to imagine how you will respond to various problems: the chickens get loose, the exploding envelope backfires, the hot-air balloon flies away. The more sophisticated your mischief, the more elaborate your plans need to be.

For complex pranks, you should have not only a backup plan, but a backup backup plan, and (in extreme cases) an *alternate* backup backup plan. "Plan A" is the name of your original plan, and backups are called "Plan B," "Plan C," and

"Plan D." Get each plan down in writing. If it's not in writing, it's just an idea, not a plan.

As you make your plans, keep all your notes, documents, maps, architectural blueprints, receipts, and check stubs in a large, plain, unmarked envelope, preferably with a string tie. A plain envelope is much better than an envelope that screams "SECRET PLANS—DO NOT OPEN" in blazing red letters.

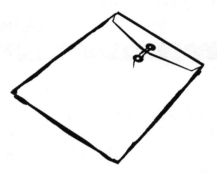

✓ Acquire a large, unmarked envelope for storing plans. The envelope should be 8.5"x11" with no markings.

KEEPING SECRETS

Psst . . . can you keep a secret?

Well, *can* you?

Secrets have a mind of their own. They *want* to be told.

"Information wants to be free." This, young prankster, is why you must learn to practice the ancient art of secret-keeping.

Secrets are precious. That's why they're secrets. Keep them that way.

When you're preparing to plant four hundred pink flamingos on the front lawn of your church, the urge to tell someone will be overwhelming. Learn to resist this temptation.

If *one wrong person* finds out what you're planning, it's all over. That's all it takes—one person. The famous bank robber Willie "the Actor" Sutton stole more than two million dollars from at least twenty banks throughout his career, engineering brilliant and daring escapes that left police scratching their heads. You know how they caught him? When other members of his team sold him down the river.

Selling someone down the river: Hurting someone who trusted you by revealing their secrets.

Let your word be gold. Never go back on it. Maintain absolute integrity at all times.

Make sure you surround yourself with people who can also keep secrets. Tell them you expect them to always keep your secrets, and be absolutely trustworthy. Hold yourself to the same standard.

> ✓ Ask a friend to tell you a secret. Keep it.
>
> WWW.MISCHIEFMAKERSMANUAL.COM

THE BUDDY SYSTEM

It is usually better to prank with a partner. At the very least, one of you can post lookout (see **How to Make a Lookout Station**, page 35) while the other makes mischief. And some pranks are so large they require a team, a band of merry pranksters. Choose your confederates carefully.

Start with a partner. Look for a friend who's trustworthy and loyal. The two of you should have **good chemistry**, which means you work well together and also that you enjoy making chemicals in labs.

The two of you should share a similar sense of humor. You should each buy a copy of this manual and read it thoroughly. Buy an extra copy, just in case. Maintain absolute secrecy at all times.

As your pranks grow more ambitious, you will need to add members to your mischief-making team. Build up your team slowly. Test out new friends on smaller pranks before moving on to more sophisticated mischief.

Definitely give your team a name.

SUGGESTED PRANK TEAM NAMES:

- Prank Team Alpha
- X-12
- **S**uper **P**ranksters **I**n **T**raining
- Tuna Quartet
- Anything ending in "Guild"

 Find a trusted partner.

HOW TO MAKE A LOOKOUT STATION

Lookouts are useful for warning of approaching danger. It's often boring to be assigned lookout, but it's important to be able to do it well. Lookouts are the first line of defense on a well-planned prank.

Lookout: Person or persons assigned to stand guard and "look out" for approaching authority figures (parents, teachers, PTA presidents, etc.). The code name for a lookout is a "sentry," since most adults do not know that word.

There are two types of lookout: **visible lookouts** and **invisible lookouts**. Visible lookouts are for situations where it's okay to be seen. For instance, let's say you and a friend are executing **The Backward Classroom** (see page 197), and you've been assigned to look out for an approaching math teacher.

1. Set both of your cell phones to "vibrate." Assign a speed-dial button to your partner, if you haven't already.

2. Stand as far away from the scene of the prank as you can get away with. You want as much advance warning as possible.

3. Stand in your assigned lookout location with the cell phone to your ear and your thumb on the speed-dial button. Stay alert; maintain vigilance.

4. If you see someone approach, simply press the speed-dial button. This will alert your partner through a vibrating cell phone that trouble is on its way. While you do this, pretend to be talking on the phone to your parents; no one ever thinks to question someone talking on a cell phone.

5. If more time is needed, you can also delay the math teacher with an algebra question.

Some pranking locations require multiple lookouts, also knows as a **Team Lookout**. Each team member should follow the instructions above, and stand in locations that allow maximum lookout coverage. If possible, use geometry (see **Figure 2**).

An **invisible lookout** functions much the same way, but

the person on lookout must first secure a good hiding place. You need a hiding place with a clear line of sight; tall windows make good vantage points, as do trees (either *in* or *behind*). When trouble approaches, remain absolutely still except for your thumb speed-dialing your partner.

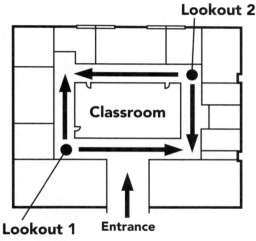

Figure 2: *Most buildings have a square or rectangle shape, also called a* **quadrilateral***. Proper quadrilateral coverage usually involves two lookouts, each covering maximum visible area.*

☑ With your partner, practice an **invisible lookout** in a safe environment, away from any active mischief (your house or neighborhood). Alert your partner when you see someone approach, using the method above as a guide.

HOW TO FLEE

Whenever you are on a dangerous pranking mission, you should constantly be on the lookout for an escape. Never let your guard down. But you must also stay relaxed enough to carry off the mischief and have fun. This balance of staying **alert but relaxed** is key to the delicate art of mischief making.

There are two ways to escape:

1. **Hauling.** Just run like the wind. Most adults are fat and sluggish, since they live on a diet of McDonald's and gravy. If you stay in good shape, you can easily outrun them. This is why the disciplined prankster does aerobic exercises three times a week for thirty to forty-five minutes (see **Figure 3**).

2. **Walking away briskly.** Running away can seem suspicious. Sometimes you can flee by just walking away, but to do this properly *you have to trust that no one is following you.* Resist the urge to look back and stare. You don't want anyone to see your face, which could be used to identify you later in a lineup.

A NOTE ABOUT BEING CHASED:
Not fun. Try to avoid it.

☑ Go to a coffee shop (Starbucks or similar) and shout, "HALF-PRICE CAPPUCCINO FOR EVERYONE!" Then flee.

FIGURE 3: THE PRANKSTER'S WORKOUT

Exercise A: *Running*

Exercise B: *Evading*

Exercise C: *Tumbling*

Exercise D: *Climbing Fences*

DIVERSIONS

Diversions are used to direct attention away from mischief being made in another location. They're often as fun and enjoyable as the prank itself, which is why some pranksters choose to specialize as "Diversions Experts."

Diversions can be as creative as your imagination will allow, but use the handy *M3* DEVISE-A-DIVERSION chart to think up starting recipes.

Verbs	Containers	Preposition	Nouns
DECORATE	SWIMMING POOL	WITH	DEAD FROGS
FILL	WATER FOUNTAIN	WITH	JELL-O
STUFF	CHURCH PODIUM	WITH	SHAVING CREAM
CONCEAL	BATHTUB	WITH	SUDS
OVERFLOW	TOILETS	WITH	POST-IT NOTES

✓ Using the patented DEVISE-A-DIVERSION chart, write a one-page description of how you would pull off that diversion.

LOOKING OFFICIAL

It is an unfortunate fact of life, but a fact that you can use to your advantage, that *people generally trust appearances.* This is why the aspiring prankster always tries to look presentable. Work to blend in, not stand out. Kids with mohawks and nose rings are the first ones to get suspected when the prank hits the fan.

The best way to infiltrate the system is to *look normal.* They'll never suspect you.

UNIFORMS AND COSTUMES

Every good prankster has a Basic Black wardrobe (page 42), plus any number of specialty costumes (pages 44-49). Your parents will be so surprised to hear you take an interest in clothes that they will probably buy these items with very little pestering.

SIMPLE COSTUMES ARE YOUR BEST BUY

Often, a simple costume can make you look like a store employee or other authority figure. **Charlie Todd**, one of the great pranksters alive today, convinced about *eighty* mischief makers to show up at a Best Buy store in New York City wearing a blue shirt and khaki pants. They looked so similar to actual Best Buy employees that customers couldn't tell the difference, and the store managers freaked.

THE BASIC BLACK

All-purpose prankster's wardrobe, "normal" enough to wear to school, but provides excellent camouflage at night. Basic Black is the mischief maker's uniform.

1. Clean dark jeans (dark blue or black)
2. Plain dark T-shirt (no logos or artwork)
3. Plain dark sweatshirt (no hood)
4. Ball cap
5. Good-quality digital watch (with timer if possible)
6. Good-quality running shoes (black, nonreflective)

WARNING: Never wear sunglasses. Too suspicious.

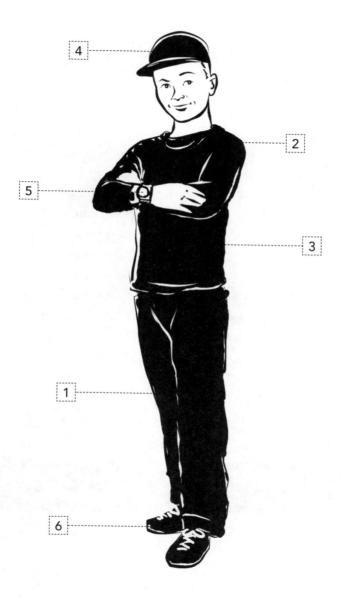

THE POWER SUIT

A suit makes you look like you're in charge. People trust somebody in a suit. But suits should only be worn when pranking an important event: weddings, funerals, the Super Bowl, etc. Suits can also be used to help you impersonate the leader of an important event or organization.

Depending on your circumstance, a suit might be overkill (although it never hurts to wear one to church). If you do go the "suit route," try to get your parents to buy your suit from a reputable men's store. Ask the clerk's opinion, not your parents. When they ask why you want a suit, tell them, "I just think it's about time I owned a suit." It's very difficult for parents to argue with this.

1. Suit pants or slacks
2. White cotton undershirt
3. Dress shirt
4. Necktie
5. Sport coat (also called "suit coat" or "blazer")
6. Dressy running shoes (Rockports preferred)

WARNING: Never wear bow ties, clip-on ties, or bolo ties.

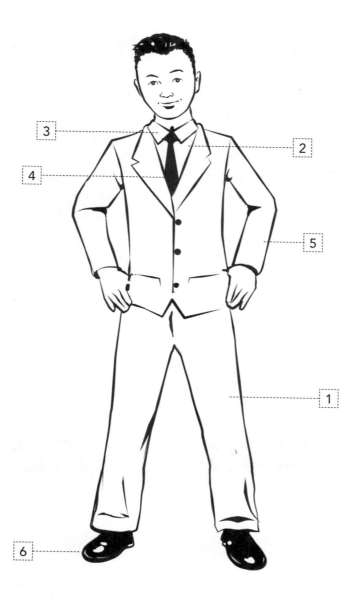

THE PAPERBOY

People trust a paperboy. The trick is to make a messenger bag that looks like it's from your local big-city newspaper. This isn't difficult; just take the logo from their website, and use it to customize a messenger bag at www.cafepress.com. An official logo makes you more believable.

This costume is useful because the messenger bag can be used to carry very heavy items over long distances. You can be trudging through somebody's backyard with a messenger bag full of vanilla custard and dead frogs, and people will go, "Oh, it's just the paperboy."

If by chance you run into a *real* paperboy, do not panic. Just nod and walk away briskly.

1. Clean dark jeans (dark blue or black)
2. Striped T-shirt (no logos or artwork)
3. Good-quality messenger bag (with logo if possible)
4. A few newspapers (date does not matter)
5. Running shoes

NOTE: If you're *actually a paperboy*, all the better.

THE CRAZY COSTUME

Sometimes the sneakiest costume is the most outrageous one. With a little planning, a "Crazy Costume" can get you into any party or sporting event. People love the idea of the Crazy Costume, and will often give you access to places you couldn't otherwise go (sporting events, rock concerts, monster truck rallies). You can just start marching in any parade, and no one will stop you. You haven't lived until you've worn a Crazy Costume at least once.

Most cities have a **costume shop**, a fantastic and wonderful place where they have a wide array of hilarious costumes that you can usually rent by the day (Google "costume shop" and your zip code to find the closest one).

The best Crazy Costume looks like a furry mascot of some sort. Make sure it completely covers your body, and has a full costume head (instead of just a mask). An animal costume (chicken, cow, gopher, etc.) is a good alternate choice, but not those two-person cow costumes, which just look silly.

A friend should act as your "helper" or "guide," especially since you usually can't see really well through the head.

1. Lightweight pants or shorts (it gets hot in there)
2. Comfortable T-shirt
3. Ridiculous-looking costume
4. Customized T-shirt (instant mascot)
5. Running shoes

THE PRANKSTER'S TOOL KIT

You won't build your tool kit overnight, but be on the lookout for these items when you're on a trip to Wal-Mart; sometimes you can just slip an item in the basket for your parents to buy you.

1. High-quality digital watch (with timer, if possible)
2. Swiss Army knife (or equivalent)
3. Durable flashlight (make sure it can withstand a drop from at least five feet)
4. Headlamp (hands-free flashlight; very useful for nighttime mischief)
5. Clipboard (good for organizing; people always trust a clipboard)
6. String-tie envelope (useful for storing plans)
7. Cell phone (required features: digital camera, text messaging, vibrating ring)
8. Small tool kit (just explain, "Dad, I'm tired of using your tools," which usually works)
9. Good-quality backpack (be sure it contains lots of hidden pockets)

> ☑ Assemble the Basic Black wardrobe, and three items from the Prankster's Tool Kit.

SIGNATURES

Signatures make things look official. They can be used for very funny pranks by printing up ridiculous signs that contain a small notice such as DO NOT REMOVE THIS SIGN UNDER PENALTY OF LAW, accompanied by a random signature.

WARNING:

EATING THIS FOOD MAY
CAUSE MUD BUTT

DO NOT REMOVE THIS SIGN UNDER PENALTY OF LAW.

SIGNED, _Daryl Rhea_

This one is useful for school cafeterias, Starbucks, etc.

DO NOT ENTER!
ASBESTOS REMOVAL

THIS SIGN MAY NOT BE REMOVED FOR TEN DAYS.

SIGNED, _Pepe Roni_

This is a fail-safe method for keeping people out of rooms while you're making mischief. Asbestos is a building material that can cause severe illness. Adults in particular are afraid of it.

Everyone should know a few signatures. Make up a few funny names like "I.P. Freely" or "Bea O'Problem," then practice signing them, getting the hang of signing a name that's not your own. Use one of these ridiculous signatures whenever you're asked to sign something ridiculous, like a wedding guest book or school petition.

DO NOT REMOVE THIS SIGN

SIGNED, *Ivan Oder*

See how many of these you can hang up before they start taking them down.

☑ Practice writing three funny names, at least ten times each.

E-MAIL ACCOUNTS

Every good prankster has two or three e-mail accounts (see **Top Three Free Online E-Mail Services** for a list of providers). They're easy to create using free online e-mail services, and they're easy to abandon.

When you prank people by e-mail, you have a digital record of what happened. It's like a court transcript. Your prank lives on forever.

Prank e-mail accounts come in handy when you begin pranking companies, or when you need to send a prank e-mail to the president or the prime minister of England. Definitely write your rabbi from the prank account, assuming your rabbi can take the joke.

Prank e-mail is very difficult to trace, but you should always exercise caution and common sense to make sure you don't get caught. Check prank accounts only when you think you might have mail, and avoid logging in otherwise. Don't leave a trail. Use the Firefox web browser instead of Internet Explorer, and "Clear Private Data" at the end of each session (Ctrl+Shift+Del), which will erase your history.

Do not forward prank e-mails to your primary e-mail account. It's too easy to accidentally *respond from* your central e-mail account, revealing your true identity. This can be disastrous.

It is best to memorize all passwords instead of writing them down.

TOP THREE FREE ONLINE E-MAIL SERVICES

1. Gmail (www.gmail.com)
2. AIM Mail (webmail.aol.com)
3. Yahoo Mail (mail.yahoo.com)

PRANK PHONE CALLS

"Moe's Bar and Grill."

"Is Seymour there?"

"Who?"

"First name Seymour. Last name Butz."

"Just a sec, I'll check. HEY, EVERYBODY! Is there a BUTZ here? A *Seymour Butz*? Hey, everybody, *I WANNA SEYMOUR BUTZ!*"

While Bart Simpson is the most well-known prank phone caller of our time, he comes from a long and proud line of pranksters, dating back to Alexander Graham Bell, the inventor of the telephone (see **History's First Phone Call: A Prank?**).

Prank calls (also called "crank calls," "phony phone calls," or "wind-ups" if you live in England) are fun because the person on the other side of the phone *can't see your face*, so they can't tell that you and your partner are laughing to the point of near-choking.

THREE RULES OF PRANK PHONE CALLING

RULE #1: Avoid caller ID. Caller ID is the prankster's worst enemy. When you're making a mischievous phone call, you don't want it tracked back to your cell phone or (worse yet) *your parents' house*. To "block" caller ID, so your number doesn't appear on their phone, **dial *67 before dialing the number**.

Note that some people have **caller ID block** on their phones, which means you will not be able to dial them unless you reveal your number. Don't call these people.

HOW TO BLOCK CALLER ID

Dial *67, then the number. If you're trying to call 1-212-555-5555, dial *67-1-212-555-5555 instead.

RULE #2: Memorize a fake phone number. This comes in handy if someone asks you for your number, which happens surprisingly often, especially when you're pranking radio call-in shows. They always think this question will trick you, so be prepared. Let's say you're calling a pet shop:

YOU: Gimme some chicken! Gimme some *friiiied* chicken!

PET STORE OWNER: What? Who is this?

YOU: Bea O'Problem, baby! Call me Bea! I wants me some *friiiied* chicken!

PET STORE OWNER: Is this a joke? What number are you calling from?

YOU: 617-555-1212.

In this case, your real number was 617-555-2121. Switching around a few numbers, and memorizing the *switched number*, will let you always give out a fake number with confidence.

If you're ambitious, you can memorize the number for your

local Starbucks, and give this out instead. Be sure to only give fake numbers for places where you've received bad service.

A fake number is also useful if some weirdo in a convertible stops you on the street and asks for your phone number. Stay away from weirdos in convertibles.

HISTORY'S FIRST PHONE CALL: A PRANK?

Some experts think the first call may have been a *prank* call. Alexander Graham Bell, working in his laboratory with his assistant Thomas Watson, had built a machine capable of transmitting sound over a wire, using battery acid to conduct the sound. While Watson was in the other room, listening for sound to be transmitted through the exciting new device, Bell pretended to knock over a beaker of battery acid. The inventor screamed into the phone, "MR. WATSON, COME HERE! I WANT TO SEE YOU!"

Frightened by the sound of the strange new device *talking to him*, Watson came running as fast as he could, only to find Bell doubled over with laughter. "Why would I have called you *Mister* Watson?" he chortled. "What are you, royalty? Ha-ha! What a chump!"

Some historians claim this was not a prank phone call, but in fact Bell really did spill battery acid on himself. These historians have no sense of humor.

RULE #3: Don't be a pest. Most adults are busy, and will not care about a prank phone call or two. It's not worth their time. When you call them back *again and again*, they'll usually get mad, and then they'll try to catch you. Never return to the scene of a prank.

✓ Be able to explain to a partner the Three Rules of Prank Phone Calling.

WWW.MISCHIEFMAKERSMANUAL.COM

CHARACTER-BASED CALLS

Some phony phone calls are based on a character that you create ahead of time. There are three types of characters:

1. **High-status characters.** This is where you try to get authority over the person being pranked. Examples of high-status characters include Army Sergeant and Angry Customer.

YOU: I was in your *store* today, sir, and *the fish department stank*!

STORE MANAGER: I'm sorry? Who is this?

YOU: I'm a customer who was overwhelmed by the *stink* of your *fish*! It smelled like a *trash can* full of *tuna*!

STORE MANAGER: Is this a joke?

YOU: A *joke*?! I would not joke about tuna *trash-can stank* like I experienced today! *Let me speak with your supervisor!*

---

2 **Low-status characters.** This is where you act really weak and pathetic, and let the person you're pranking feel sorry for you. Examples include Mousy Man and Dying Patient.

YOU: Ohhh, my nasal passages are burning. I was in your *store* today and nearly *overcome* by the stink of your fish department, which is aggravating my fish allergies. [Sneezing, coughing]

STORE MANAGER: I'm sorry? Who is this?

YOU: Ohhh, Fnerdly McGee. Oh, my aching, sneezing, dripping nose. Oh, how those fish stank. Kerchoo.

STORE MANAGER: Is this a joke?

YOU: Ohhh, my groin hurts also. One of your fish bit me in the groin.

---

3 **Deadpan characters.** This is where you call and act totally normal, but with an outrageous question or problem. You should completely act like *your* universe is normal, and *theirs* is the screwed-up one.

YOU: I have an unusual request. I'd like to buy your stinkiest fish.

STORE MANAGER: I'm sorry? Who is this?

YOU: My name is Mike, and I know this sounds strange, but it's for a science project. Do you think you could do that?

STORE MANAGER: Is this a joke?

YOU: Not a joke at all. What I need you to do is put your face down *real close* next to each of your fish, and choose the one that smells the stinkiest.

STORE MANAGER: Hmm. Well, okay, hang on…

YOU: Sniff each one ten or twelve times if you can.

Give your characters names, and practice them with your partner. If they're funny enough to make you laugh when you're practicing them over a cell phone, they'll be funny enough to *kill* when you're pulling a prank call.

Try not to practice your character around your family. They'll think it's weird.

FAMOUS PRANK PHONE CALLERS

- Jimmy Kimmel
- David Letterman
- Ashton Kutcher
- The Jerky Boys
- Your parents (when they were your age)

 Develop a character and practice it with a partner.

SOUNDBOARDS

Soundboards are a collection of sound files that play on your computer, usually movie quotes from a celebrity. The person on the other end thinks they're talking to a real person, but you're actually just playing random quotes from Will Ferrell or Paris Hilton. Nine times out of ten soundboards just end up confusing the person. But the tenth person will fall for it completely, which is comedy gold.

To find soundboards, just Google "soundboards" for tons of free and hilarious options. These are some of the easiest prank phone calls to make, because *you don't even have to talk*!

POPULAR SOUNDBOARD THEMES

SOUNDBOARD	SAMPLE QUOTE
Arnold Schwarzenegger	"I'm a cop, you idiot!"
Napoleon Dynamite	"Tina! Come get some ham!"
Will Ferrell	"Sweat glands!"
Paris Hilton	"Hi," "Yeah," and "That's hot."

☑ Try out a soundboard on your computer or laptop.

WHAT TO DO IF THEY CALL BACK

Pick up the phone. If you follow the rules above, you should be safe from callbacks. But if they do manage to track you down, make sure you *don't let them get to your voice mail or answering machine.* Quickly answer the phone, then quietly stuff it under a pillow. Eventually they'll hang up. Don't pick it up again for a long time.

If they continue to call back, make sure you're prepared with *M3* **Emergency Soundboards**, which are free downloadable sound files that play through your computer speakers, and will usually get rid of even the most stubborn caller. These soundboards are free for all *M3* members.

M3 EMERGENCY SOUNDBOARDS	
SOUNDBOARD	**DESCRIPTION**
Fax Tone	A screeching fax tone that will play indefinitely
Angry Parent	"I'm really sorry about this, my kid has been playing around with the phone, and it won't happen again. I apologize. Excuse me, I've got to go take care of this. [*Click*]"
Prerecorded Error Message	"We're sorry, the number you have dialed is not in service."

Keep in mind, these emergency soundboards *should only be used as a last resort.* Practice the **Three Rules of Prank Phone Calling** (see page 55) at all times.

☑ Download *M3* Emergency Soundboards to your computer or laptop at:
www.mischiefmakersmanual.com/tools/soundboards/

REVERSE PRANK PHONE CALLS

Occasionally you get lucky: The phone will ring, and when you answer it, it's someone who called the wrong number. That's the best time to make a prank call, because they will never expect it.

You really have to think fast. You need to immediately launch into one of your **Characters** (see page 58) or a similar comedy routine.

Usually the person will ask to speak with someone (for instance: "Is Bob there?").

You'll say, "Who?" because that's everybody's natural response to a wrong number.

"Bob," they'll say.

"Oh, BOB," you should say, then put your hand to the phone.

One approach is to call loudly for Bob, again and again, getting more and more frustrated. Then make up some excuse for why Bob can't come to the phone: "He's playing with his Barbie collection," or "Bob can't come to the phone, he's got explosive diarrhea." Always be sure to use the name, this makes it more believable.

Another approach is to wait for a moment, then come back on the phone and pretend to be Bob. The pause while you're "passing the phone" to Bob can be used to prepare your character.

If, by chance, the person calls you back by hitting *69, then use *M3* **Emergency Soundboards** (page 62).

✓ Have a partner pretend to call you with a "wrong number" call. Improvise the prank conversation that would follow.

GETTING AWAY WITH STUFF

Unbelievably, there are some days actually *set aside* for pranking. These days are few and far between, so make sure you begin planning well in advance.

APRIL FOOL'S DAY

An *entire day* devoted to pranking and mischief. *What were they thinking?*

It's almost too good to be true, but it *is*, and it comes around once a year. April one. April Fool's Day is the perfect day for carrying out really ambitious mischief (see **Experts Only**, page 189).

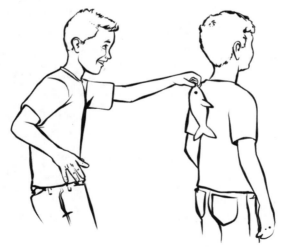

How kids in France celebrate April Fool's Day

It is not just your right, it is your *duty* to prank on April 1.

In **Scotland**, April Fool's Day was once known as Hunting the Gowk, which means "hunting the cuckoo," or "hunting for an easy target to prank."

In **France**, April Fool's Day is called *poisson d'avril* (literally "April fish"), and the big joke is to try to stick a paper fish onto your victim's back without being noticed.

In **Denmark**, they celebrate April Fool's Day on April 1, and an identical day called *Maj-kat* on May 1. Danish kids get *double the pranks*!

HALLOWEEN

Though not as widely recognized as April Fool's Day, Halloween is still a well-known night for pranking. Follow the **Prankster's Code** (page 23), and you will greatly improve your chances of staying out of trouble.

Pumpkin pranks. One sad Halloween tradition is to smash a pumpkin, an act of vandalism from which the band Smashing Pumpkins gets its name. Smashing pumpkins is acceptable if you use a **Catapult** (page 157) and your own pumpkin. Otherwise look for more creative pumpkin pranks (see **The Roaming Gnome**, page 200, or **Suds Mountain**, page 240). Don't **Damage, Deface, or Destroy** (page 25).

Toilet paper pranks. Less-talented pranksters will sometimes toilet-paper someone's yard (also known as "TPing someone's yard"), by throwing rolls of toilet paper into trees and bushes because it looks bad and is difficult to clean up. Why not be creative instead? Why not fill their entire *car* with wadded-up toilet paper? The shock the next morning is just as great, but the car is easier to clean up.

Smashing pumpkins using a catapult

Costume pranks. Halloween costumes provide interesting opportunities for pranking (see **Crazy Costume**, page 48). One costume stunt is to dress up like a scarecrow and then sit on your porch, very still. It helps if you have a rocking chair or some other seat you can flop into, so you look more like a scarecrow. When trick-or-treaters come to the door, you leap up and shout, "Boo!" and they wet their pants.

Ring the doorbell and run. Instead of saying "trick or treat," you ring the doorbell, then tear off. This one's pretty much a classic.

LAST DAY OF SCHOOL

The last day of school is very dangerous for adults, and very good for kids. The balance of power shifts completely. Everybody knows that once that bell rings, you're leaving, maybe for good. You're out of there like a millionaire. In the words of the great poet Alice Cooper, "School's out for summer."

On the last day of school, they can't catch you. What are they going to make you do, come back and *repeat the last day*? The teachers want out of there as badly as you do, probably worse. They just want to relax by the pool for three months, and get you monsters out of their hair.

That's why, as soon as the bell rings, it's like an invisible cloak of invincibility falls down around you. You are free to create masterful mountains of mind-blowing mischief.

Just be sure to get out of there as quickly as possible. You don't want to have to repeat seventh grade.

☑ Memorize the three holidays of pranking: April Fool's Day (April 1), Halloween (October 31), and the last day of school (you'll have to look it up).

PRANK RANK ACHIEVED!

Congratulations, young prankster. Completing all the exercises in the previous section means that you have now mastered the second level of mischief. You have earned the title of **First-Class Mischief Maker.**

☑ Visit www.mischiefmakersmanual.com to track progress and download badge.

DOUBLE MUD BUTT
Brownies
RECIPE 2

ex-lax

In the next section, you will learn how to pull off **prank moves**, or simple stunts using low-cost items you probably already have lying around the house. These are the building blocks of more complicated pranks, so learn them well, grasshopper. You have learned much, but much there still is to learn.

PRANK MOVES

There are certain "classic" pranks that every mischief maker should know. Even if you never pull them, you should understand how they work, in case anyone pulls them on *you*.

The following pranks work well at home, but they're also great for summer camp, vacation homes, or anywhere you have access to someone's living space.

THE APPLE-PIE BED

This prank dates back hundreds of years, and is truly a classic, like the pastry it is named after. It's named The Apple-Pie Bed because it makes the inside of the bed resemble an apple turnover folded on itself.

An apple turnover

An Apple-Pie Bed

The modern term for this prank is "short-sheeting a bed," and it's extremely simple. With a partner, and some practice, it can be done in less than a minute. You can do it by yourself as well.

The Apple-Pie Bed is a good prank to know, because *everyone sleeps*. It's especially effective for your parents on their anniversary.

How to Make The Apple-Pie Bed:

You will need:		
• A bed		
Money required:		**Time required:**
Free		A few minutes
Success rate:	95 percent	**Mischief level:** 1

Most beds have a fitted sheet (that you sleep *on*), a top sheet (that you sleep *under*), and one or more blankets/comforters/dirty underwear.

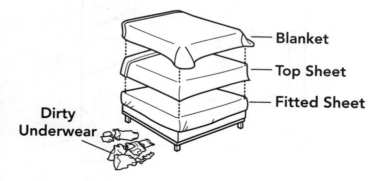

Blanket

Top Sheet

Fitted Sheet

Dirty Underwear

1 First, make a mental note of where everything on the bed is placed.

2 Take off all the covers and the top sheet (leaving only the fitted sheet).

3 Lay the top sheet back out on the bed. Tuck the *top side* snugly under the mattress.

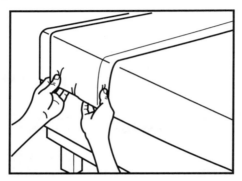

4 Now take the *bottom* two corners of the sheet, and fold them so they're about a foot from the top of the bed. By folding the sheet in half, you're forming a "pie pocket."

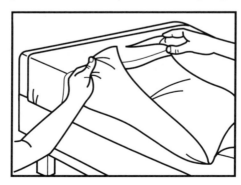

5 Put the rest of the covers, comforters, and dirty underwear back on the bed, exactly as they were when you found them. Try to make sure the sheet is showing, so they can easily grab it to crawl inside.

Note: Some sheets have a different color on the reverse side. If the top layer looks suspicious, you can turn it down so that the front side is showing.

One variation on The Apple-Pie Bed is to add *whole apples* to their bed, for that authentic apple turnover taste. This is not recommended on your parents' anniversary.

> ✓ With the help of a partner, practice The Apple-Pie Bed on one of your own beds. Then make the bed look normal. Be sure your parents notice that you made your bed without being asked.
>
> WWW.MISCHIEFMAKERSMANUAL.COM

THE INVISIBLE TOILET FORCE FIELD

For years, scientists have been developing a material that can be used to create an invisible "force field" across the seat of a toilet. Here's how it works: Your dad or sister goes to use the bathroom in the middle of the night, and everything *looks* normal, but the advanced force field technology sends crazy droplets of pee spraying everywhere, like deflector shields on a futuristic spacecraft.

Thanks to the hard work of these noble scientists, chemists, and marketing executives, we now have this "toilet force field technology" in a package you probably already have in your kitchen drawer.

It's called Saran Wrap.

The scientists couldn't reveal its true purpose, so they disguised it as a "plastic wrap" to keep food fresh. *Their trick worked!* Your parents have been buying it for years, unaware of its true purpose. It's transparent and sticky, which makes it useful for a variety of pranks (see **It's a Wrap**, page 82).

How to Make the Invisible Toilet Force Field:

You will need:	
• Toilet • Saran Wrap	• Scissors (optional)
Money required:	**Time required:**
Free	A few minutes
Success rate: 55 percent	**Mischief level:** 2

Most toilets have a cover, a seat, and the toilet itself.

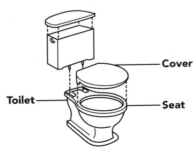

1. Lift the cover and the top seat.
2. Grab a sheet of plastic wrap and stretch it across the opening of the toilet.
3. Stretch the plastic sheet until it is perfectly smooth, then put on a second layer right next to it. The two layers should overlap just enough to keep a tight seal.
4. Put down the seat, but leave the cover open.

Step 3

Step 4

5. Smooth down the plastic wrap onto the bowl. Trim with scissors for a polished, professional look.
6. Be sure to wash your hands afterward. You've been touching toilets all day.

Step 5

Step 6

IT'S A WRAP

- Saran Wrap can be used to turn nearly *anything* into a plastic cocoon: televisions, refrigerators, steering wheels, *Harry Potter* novels, iPods, everything in and on a desk, the desk itself, etc.
- Don't wrap anything that's alive, with the possible exception of large houseplants.
- Instead of Saran Wrap, you can also wrap things in **aluminum foil** for a cool, space-age look.

SNAKE SNATCHER

Most mischief makers own some kind of rubber bug, snake, or giant fly, but very few know how to properly use them. These pranks are a lot more disturbing if they *suddenly dart across the floor or yard*, preferably right in front of someone important, like the president of the local Rotary Club.

The trick is **fishing line**, which is practically invisible, making it much better than regular string. Fishing line is easy to find at Wal-Mart, or you may already have some in the garage.

How to pull off Snake Snatcher:

You will need:			
• Giant rubber snake		• Fishing line	
Money required:		**Time required:**	
Less than $10.00		A few minutes	
Success rate:	50 percent	**Mischief level:**	2

1 │ Take a huge rubber snake (or spider, frog, large cockroach, etc.). Find a good location for the prank (doorways work well, or behind tables).

2 │ Tie fishing line around the fake snake. Depending on the shape of the snake, you may be able to tie it behind the head. Otherwise, poke a hole through the snake, using a pick or sharp object. Thread the fishing line through the hole.

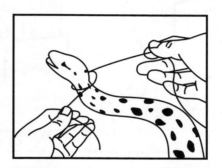

3 │ Set the prank. Put the snake in its hiding spot, and thread the fishing line to your hiding spot. Don't worry if the snake is not perfectly hidden; they won't be looking for it.

4 Yank the prank. Just before someone walks over the line, yank the snake toward you while remaining absolutely silent. Do not give away your position by screaming.

VARIATIONS

- As you yank the snake across the floor, get a friend to run after it, yelling loudly, as if it has escaped. A butterfly net wouldn't hurt.
- Get a friend to yell, "HAS ANYONE SEEN MY SNAKE?" from the other room, a minute before you yank the snake across the floor.
- The Double Whammy: You and a friend cross-yank two snakes across your target's path, making it seem like a plague. WARNING: Do not get lines crossed. Follow diagram carefully.

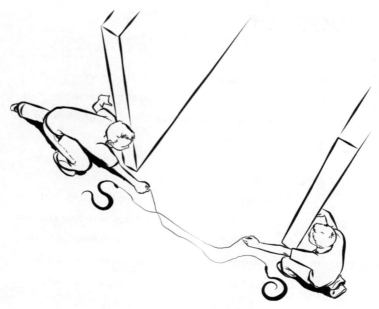

The Double Whammy

FOOD FUN

Everyone eats. That makes eating the perfect opportunity for mischief, especially at large communal gatherings like picnics and church potlucks, where it's difficult to pin it on a single person.

SALT AND PEPPER SWITCHEROO

Be on the lookout for those glass saltshakers with the metal screw-on lids. Some mischief makers unscrew the lids, then leave them *resting* on the top of the saltshaker. When someone goes to salt their food, they get a plateful of salt.

A more clever twist is to *switch* the salt and pepper, so they shake the *opposite*. When they go to put *salt* on their corn, they'll shake *pepper* instead. If you have saltshakers that you can't see through, this is easy—just dump the salt and pepper onto two pieces of paper, then carefully pour them back into the *wrong* containers.

If you have glass saltshakers, there's a more impressive version of this prank that makes it *look* like there's salt in the saltshaker—but pepper comes out the top!

How to Pull off the Salt and Pepper Switcheroo:

You will need:	
• Salt and pepper shakers	• Two pieces of paper
• Saran Wrap	• Scissors
Money required:	**Time required:**
Free	15 minutes
Success rate: 75 percent	**Mischief level:** 3

1. Unscrew the salt and pepper shakers.
2. Dump out half the salt and half the pepper onto two separate pieces of paper.
3. Tear off a sheet of Saran Wrap about the length of your index finger.
4. Fold the Saran Wrap in half, then poke the middle of the Saran Wrap down into the opening of the saltshaker, forming a kind of "pocket" to hold the pepper. Push it in with your finger, about an inch.
5. Pour the pepper into the pocket.
6. Screw the lid back on. Do it very gently, so you don't tear the Saran Wrap. You want *just enough* to secure the lid, no more.
7. Carefully trim away the excess Saran Wrap on the outside, so the trick is invisible. Give it a shake to test it.

The Switcheroo prank can also be modified to work on different foods (imagine reversing a bottle of mustard and a container of ketchup). It's always good to wash the containers after you've emptied them, before you fill them with the wrong substance. A funnel comes in handy also.

 Be able to explain the steps of the Salt and Pepper Switcheroo to a partner.

WWW.MISCHIEFMAKERSMANUAL.COM

EGG IN THE MILK

Picture this: You're at the table, calmly sipping a glass of milk. Suddenly you feel something *hard* and *strange* hit your lip. When you look down, you don't see anything except white milk.

For a few seconds, this is absolutely confusing, and slightly scary. *Was it ice? What was that thing? Wait a minute . . . is that . . . ewww, what **is** that thing? Frank, there's something **white** and **hard** in my milk! Is it a billiard ball? What the . . . oh, I don't believe it.*

It's at this point that the pranked person realizes *it's just a hard-boiled egg.*

Watching someone's confusion, shock, disgust, realization, and then laughter at Egg in the Milk is pretty much the classic prank reaction. When it goes as planned, it's just enormously fun to watch.

How to Pull off Egg in the Milk:

You will need:	
• Hard-boiled egg	• Milk
Money required:	**Time required:**
Free	A few minutes
Success rate: 85 percent	**Mischief level:** 1

1. Tell your parents you're interested in trying hard-boiled eggs, and ask if they'll make a couple for you. You can also hard-boil your own (cover the eggs with cold water, then bring them to a boil for ten minutes).

2. After the egg has cooked, allow it to cool completely.

3. Before a meal, gently drop the egg into the pranked glass of milk.

4. Serve and enjoy.

NOTES:

- Works better in a cup than a glass. Cups hide the egg better.
- The stunt doesn't work if they're using a straw. It also doesn't work if they don't usually drink milk. They have to be expecting regular milk.

✓ Cook and eat a hard-boiled egg. They're a good source of protein.

STAPLER IN THE JELL-O

Jell-O is one of the best ingredients for mischief making. It's colorful, harmless, and you can eat the prank later. If you don't have some in your pantry already, Jell-O can be found in the "Baking Needs" aisle at the supermarket. Be sure to use Jell-O *gelatin*, not Jell-O *pudding*. Pudding is good for dropping from hot-air balloons. Totally different prank.

The classic Jell-O prank is to make a stapler appear in the middle of a quivering Jell-O dessert, with the stapler frozen in time like a museum exhibit. This works best if you're giving the Jell-O as a gift, and it's their stapler.

Instead of a stapler, you can substitute other objects, like a favorite coffee mug or a picture of your sister. Get creative. Jell-O goes with so many things.

ALWAYS BE CAREFUL:

- Don't use anything that will be ruined by Jell-O (anything that can't get wet).
- Avoid anything too small (choking hazard).
- Don't use anything of great sentimental value.
- It's best to wash the object first.

How to Pull off Stapler in the Jell-O:

You will need:	
• Stapler • Jell-O (at least 3 boxes of the same flavor)	• Saran Wrap
Money required:	**Time required:**
Less than $5.00	Several hours
Success rate: 40 percent	**Mischief level:** 4

1 Find a bowl big enough to hold the stapler. Line the bowl completely with Saran Wrap, which will help you pull the Jell-O out of the bowl when it's finished.

2 Mix one box of Jell-O according to instructions. Yellow Jell-O is best, and not just because it rhymes. Red, orange, or green Jell-O will also work. You can also buy *clear* gelatin, for a weird futuristic look.

3 Pour three inches of Jell-O into the bowl, and put it into the refrigerator for at least three hours. While it sets, make two more boxes of Jell-O.

4 Take the solid Jell-O out of the fridge. Place the stapler (or object) on top, and pour the rest of the liquid Jell-O on top. Put in the fridge overnight.

5 Get a large, decorative plate or serving tray. The fancier the better. Take the finished Jell-O out of the fridge, and turn it upside down on the serving tray.

7 Use the Saran Wrap to "guide" the mold out of the bowl. Once it's positioned correctly, carefully unpeel the Saran Wrap from the Jell-O. Take your time with this step. If the Jell-O breaks, the prank is ruined.

8 Serve and enjoy. (Or just leave it in the fridge to be found.)

✓ Be sure your pantry is stocked with Jell-O. If not, ask your parents to pick some up at the store.

BATHROOM BASICS

Bathroom pranks are useful because *everybody uses the bathroom.* The president uses the bathroom. Ex-presidents use the bathroom. Your preacher or rabbi, your parents, each of your teachers, and your principal all use the bathroom. Think of your favorite movie star or rock singer. He or she uses the bathroom anywhere between five to seven times a day. A little more around the holidays.

This means that bathrooms are *everywhere:* home, school, your church or synagogue, restaurants, airports, and every Starbucks in America. Bathrooms are also ideal for mischief because you can have privacy in a bathroom. That's rare. Also, bathrooms have *drawers* and *cabinets* for hiding things.

You can have a lot of fun in a bathroom.

THE EERIE FOAMING TOILET

Meet your two friends, Mr. Vinegar and Mr. Baking Soda.

They're cheap, easy to purchase, and completely safe. But when put together in the right place, at the right time, they're *completely surprising and unexpected*, creating a volcano of harmless foam through the chemical reaction explained at right.

One example of a surprising time to encounter vinegar and soda is when you flush the toilet. The prank works like this: They walk into the bathroom, which has been freshly cleaned. Everything sparkles: the sink, the mirror, the commode. So it seems natural that there is white residue in the toilet—it must be leftover toilet cleaner. Of course, it's *baking soda*, and when they try to flush it away, it erupts in a *fountain of froth.*

$$CH_3COOH + NaHCO_3 \rightarrow NaCH_3COO + H_2O + CO_2$$

(VINEGAR) + (BAKING SODA) → (SODIUM ACETATE) + (WATER) + (CARBON DIOXIDE)

Combining vinegar with soda causes a chemical reaction resulting in:

- Sodium acetate (the chemical that gives salt-and-vinegar chips their flavor)
- Water
- Carbon dioxide

It is the fizzy carbon dioxide escaping through the water that gives the baking soda its "foam."

How to Pull off the Eerie Foaming Toilet:

You will need:	
• 2-5 huge jugs of vinegar (biggest you can find) • 1 giant box of baking soda (biggest you can find)	• Rubber gloves • Toilet brush • Cleaning supplies

Money required:		Time required:	
Less than $10.00		15 minutes	
Success rate:	75 percent	**Mischief level:**	4

1 Take the lid off the tank.

2 Flush the toilet to clear it. Make note of the sound of water refilling the tank.

3 Shut off the water to the toilet. On most toilets, this can be done with a knob between the toilet and the wall. Find the knob and turn it all the way closed.

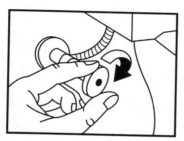

4 Flush the toilet again. You'll know the water supply is shut off if you don't hear the tank refilling.

5 Hold the handle down until the tank drains as much as possible.

6 Fill the tank back up with vinegar. You really need a lot of vinegar: at least one huge jug, two if possible. Replace the lid to the tank.

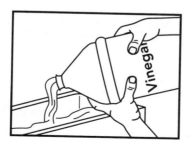

7 | Scoop out the remaining water from the bowl.

8 | Now pour your baking soda into the bowl. Using a toilet brush, work it around to a nice paste. Clean under the rim. Baking soda is one of the best all-natural cleaners, so you're actually doing them a favor by scrubbing their toilet.

9 | Clean the rest of the bathroom. This will provide an excellent cover. Leave the toilet seat down, and wait for the chaos to ensue.

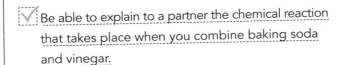

☑ Be able to explain to a partner the chemical reaction that takes place when you combine baking soda and vinegar.

WWW.MISCHIEFMAKERSMANUAL.COM

EGGHEAD

Here's a quick, simple household prank: *Replace somebody's shampoo with raw egg.* Raw eggs are disgusting and slimy. They feel like cold snot oozing over your head. And yet, you can easily clean up afterward, making it difficult for anybody to get too mad about it.

This prank is combined with making breakfast for the person who will later get egged, which is a nice touch that ties together the "egg" theme in a classy way.

How to Pull off the Egghead:

You will need:	
• 6-12 eggs • Shampoo bottle	• Extra shampoo container (rinsed and clean)

Money required:	Time required:
Less than $10.00	15 minutes

Success rate:	75 percent	Mischief level:	4

1 Wash your hands thoroughly.

2 In a large bowl, crack open the eggs.

3 Using two fingers of one hand, gently scoop out each yolk, one by one. Let the egg white slime through your fingers, so only the yolk remains in your hand. Imagine how this is going to feel on someone's head.

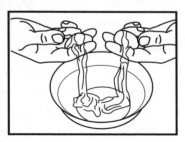

4 Put the yolks into a separate bowl. You should end up with one bowl of egg yolks and one bowl of egg whites.

5 Hide the egg whites in the refrigerator.

6 Salt and pepper the egg yolks. Add a cup of milk. With a wire whisk, beat your yolks over the sink for two minutes.

7 Heat ¼ cup cooking oil in a frying pan over medium-low heat. Pour in the eggs. Stir constantly until cooked. Serve breakfast, making sure everyone notices who helped out for a change.

8 Later, empty out the shampoo bottle into a medium-sized bowl. Rinse the bottle under hot water. (Do this at a faraway sink, as it will make a lot of bubbles.)

9 Take the chilled egg whites out of the fridge and beat twenty strokes with a fork. Using a funnel, pour the chilled egg whites into the shampoo container.

10 Using a funnel, pour the shampoo from the bowl into your alternate shampoo container.

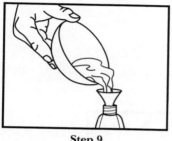

Step 9

Step 10

Most people get attached to their hair wash, so that's the reason for pouring the *real* shampoo into an alternate container. Leave it in the shower with them.

This prank also works for body soap, or anything in a squeezable container.

KETCH-UP THE BUTT

It's a prank so simple it can be performed anywhere, by anyone, at any time. It's a packet of ketchup, positioned under the toilet seat in a way that will squirt ketchup on someone's bare bottom when they sit down. Ketch-Up the Butt is also known as a "Squishy," "Toilet Squishy," or a "Loo Squishy" if you live in England.

Sometimes, the ketchup packets misfire, and instead of squirting, they *explode*. When one of these things goes off, it can release a mighty *blurt* of ketchup that reaches the bathtub, or even the next bathroom stall. The goal, however, is to *angle the packets to hit their bum*, and hope for the best. They can always wipe it off with toilet paper, after their heart rate returns to normal.

How to Set up a Successful Squishy:

1. Fold two packets of ketchup so the fat end is pointing inward, toward *their* fat end.

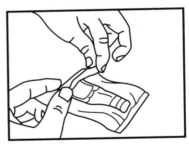

2. Place packets under the little "bumps" on the underside of the toilet seat.

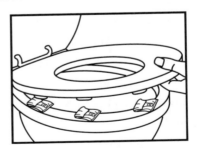

3. Put the toilet seat down. (Leave the cover up.)

SQUISHY TIPSIES

- Use packets of mustard for a colorful touch.
- Use one mustard and one ketchup for a Jackson Pollock-like flair.
- Other packaged condiments, such as relish and soy sauce, do not work well. Mayonnaise is iffy.

The biggest problem with Ketch-Up the Butt is that the ketchup packets make the toilet seat bulge up from the rim in an obvious way. But it's such an easy prank to pull that you can easily afford to set 'em up and see who sits on 'em.

☑ Set up Ketch-Up the Butt in your own home, then press down on it to gauge the reaction. Afterward, take time to clean the bathroom, so as to remove all evidence of a ketchup explosion.

WWW.MISCHIEFMAKERSMANUAL.COM

SIGN SHENANIGANS

People trust signs.

As a professional mischief maker, this works to your advantage. You can easily fool people into all kinds of crazy behavior with nothing more than a simple sign hung on a door or wall, somewhere people will notice it.

The great news is, people even trust signs that are bad and crudely drawn. A janitor can tape up a sign reading GYM CLOZED DUE TO WILD GORILA, and people will be like, "Whoa! A wild gorilla is on the loose! Run for your lives!"

Your signs should look a lot better than that. Generally speaking, the bigger and more expensive-looking a sign is, the more people will believe it. That's why this section starts with laser-printed signs (**Redesigning Signs**, page 103) and ends with instructions for **Reprogramming Signs** (page 110), which could be enough to get you mentioned on the Internet, if not the news.

The best thing about sign-related pranks is they're difficult to pin on anyone. After all: *Anyone* could have hung the sign, which leaves over six billion other suspects on planet Earth. Provided you pull off the sign prank without being seen (always use a **Lookout**, page 35), you can admire your handiwork from a safe distance. If possible, take pictures.

> ## ALWAYS BE CAREFUL
> Because people believe signs so completely, do not print anything that would harm or hurt people, either physically or mentally.

REDESIGNING SIGNS

Microsoft Word is the most commonly used computer program in the world.

This means everybody uses it. Your parents. Lawyers. The police. Gandhi used Microsoft Word. Cavemen used Microsoft Word. Adam and Eve used WordPerfect 6.2, but eventually switched to Microsoft Word.

Microsoft Word can be used to make all kinds of professional-looking documents that look *just as good as the real thing*. If you look around, many adults just use a sign printed in Word and taped in a location that's easy to see, like on a classroom door or bulletin board. If you know Word, you know as much as they do. Word is the great equalizer.

There are two main methods for making mischief with Microsoft:

1. **Copycat sign.** This is where you use Word to make an exact replica of an existing sign, but change it in some silly way. The proper time to use this prank is when someone has left a particularly ridiculous sign on the wall.

Doing a copycat sign is easy, though it takes a little time to get the details right. Take a picture of the offending sign, then fire up Microsoft Word and copy the sign's *exact formatting and font.* Your new sign really has to look *exactly like the old sign,* except for your ridiculous change.

Hang the new sign over the old one, so it's easy to remove when it's discovered by whoever's in charge. If the old sign "shows through" the new one, just use a few additional blank sheets of paper in between the two signs.

Please do not throw away your silverware!

TRASH

Copycat sign before

Please do not throw away your underwear!

TRASH

Copycat sign after

2 **Prank sign.** This is where you make up an entirely new sign, with the goal of pranking people into thinking it was left by someone important. For instance:

Dear class:
Gym class is closed today because aliens landed and ate all the balls.
Sincerely,
I.P. Freely

Putting signatures on your signs can often make them more believable (see **Signatures**, page 52). But don't overdo it—think about whether a signature would make sense. You can also add today's date, which makes it seem current.

Consider a warning in small print at the bottom of the sign. For instance, DO NOT REMOVE UNTIL _____, with a date one week in the future. Or: DO NOT REMOVE UNDER PENALTY OF PUNISHMENT.

DRIVE-THRU
DRIVE-THRU SPEAKER IS BROKEN. PLEASE YELL AS LOUDLY AS YOU CAN!

Pay careful attention to spelling and formatting. In Word, avoid the red squiggly lines, which usually mean a word is misspelled. Also look out for green squiggly lines, which usually mean a mistake in your grammar. The better your English, the more people you'll be able to fool.

Make sure your font in Word is big and readable (usually a 36- or 48-point font), and use either Arial or Times New Roman. Don't get cutesy and use Comic Sans MS, unless you're trying to imitate someone who uses Comic Sans MS a lot, in which case they deserve it.

Print your sign on the highest-quality printer you can find. Laser printers are best, but inkjet printers will also work. If you need a *really* impressive sign, you can take your Word file to your local FedEx Kinko's (or other printing shop), and ask to have your sign "dry-mounted." This will give the sign a nice stiff backing, and *everyone* will believe it.

Microsoft Word is the most important computer program for young troublemakers to learn. The best news is that if your family has a computer, it probably already has Word installed. If not, you can easily get it by telling your parents you need Word for school and other things. Don't tell them about the "other things."

☑ Use Microsoft Word to make a prank sign. Hang it up in a busy location and observe what happens.

REARRANGING SIGNS

As popularized by George Beard and Harold Hutchins of the *Captain Underpants* series, there's a famous prank where you find one of those signs with the moveable letters:

And you rearrange the letters of the sign so they read something else.

This is called an **anagram**. The classic prankster's move is to do a perfect anagram, which means no letters left over. Perfect anagrams are very difficult, which is why smart people like them. You're not after perfection, you're after pranks. Leftover letters are acceptable, as long as the new message is funny enough.

> **Anagram:** Rearranging the letters of a word or phrase to create a new word or phrase.

How to Rearrange Signs:

You will need:	
• Sign	• A ton of courage
• Ziploc bag	

Money required:	Time required:
Free	Several days

Success rate:	35 percent	Mischief level:	6

1. Find a sign with moveable letters. These generally come in two kinds: the big clear plastic letters that slide onto guides, or the pointy plastic letters that snap in and out.

2. Find a convenient time to research the sign without being noticed. Make note of any problems that will need to be creatively solved.

3. Go home and figure out your anagram. It helps to write each letter on a Post-It Note so you can play around with them. You can also use the Internet Anagram Server at **www.wordsmith.org/anagram** to suggest options.

4 Rearrange the sign. The best time to do this is not late at night, but *early in the morning*, preferably around 5:30 A.M., so your sign can greet the morning crowds. (Consider the **Paperboy** costume [page 46], since paperboys are often seen very early in the morning.)

5 In the event of leftover letters, seal them up in a large Ziploc bag, which you should tape to the side of the sign. Don't run off with the letters.

☑ Make a funny anagram of your name (first and last).
You may have up to five leftover letters.

REPROGRAMMING SIGNS

Light-up signs are attention-grabbers, which is why adults use them to display important messages . . . like school announcements and highway detours. They come in many shapes and sizes, from small **Scrolling Signs** (see **Figure 1**) to huge **Electronic Message Boards** that they have to haul in on a truck (see **Figure 2**).

PLEASE CLEAN UP AFTER YOURSELVES ...

Figure 1: *Before*

PLEASE CLEAN UP AFTER YOUR ELVES ...

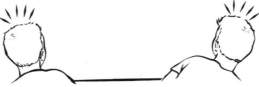

Figure 1: *After*

Figure 2: *Before*

Figure 2: *After*

Many signs have locks on their keypads. Many other signs are programmed using a detachable keyboard, and the keyboard is missing. Scrolling Signs are usually programmed with small programmable keyboards set into the device. Message boards sometimes have the password *written near the keypad*, so workers don't have to remember them. The creative prankster should always be looking for a mischievous solution to the problem that **does not Damage, Deface, or Destroy** (page 25).

How to Reprogram Electronic Signs:

You will need:	
• Sign	• Various tools
• The Internet	• Nerves of steel
Money required:	**Time required:**
Free	Several days
Success rate: 15 percent	**Mischief level:** 7

1 At a convenient time, get close enough to the sign to examine it carefully. Look for any company names or model numbers. Write these down. Look also for a manual.

2 If you didn't find a manual, then Google any names or model numbers you found. Once you find the company website, search the site for the documentation manual that matches your sign model. Most companies make these available on their websites, for free, as PDF files.

3 Memorize the manual carefully. Learn everything about it. Know the sign better than the adults who programmed it, which is usually not that hard.

4 Posting one or more **Lookouts** (see page 35), sneak to the sign and reprogram it. Again, the best time to do this, whenever possible, is early morning, before the crowds arrive. Be prepared for frequent interruptions.

5 Be sure to get a picture or video. Post it on the Internet.

☑ Do a Google search on "electronic signs" and learn more about them. Consider buying one, because electronic signs are sweet.

PRANK RANK ACHIEVED!

Congratulations, young grasshopper. You have worked your way through another level of mischief, earning yourself the title of **Minor Mischief Maker**. Wear your badge proudly. Although you are only a Minor, you're on your way to the Majors.

Visit www.mischiefmakersmanual.com to track progress and download badge.

In this section, you will learn how to build **gags**, the professional term for wacky contraptions that are used to prank people. Many of these hilarious contraptions, like Joy Buzzers and Whoopee Cushions, have been around for decades. Your education is not complete without detailed knowledge of these devices, and the best way to get detailed knowledge is to build them yourself.

You'll find step-by-step instructions in the following pages, explaining how to build these gags using everyday items you have in your kitchen or study. Some require low-cost items you can buy at Wal-Mart, Home Depot, or a drugstore.

The projects in the following pages will get progressively more difficult, but by completing each of the exercises, you will attain the level of **Major Mischief Maker**, and be one step closer to your ultimate goal: **Master Mischief Maker**. Progress you are making, young grasshopper. Progress you are making.

DO-IT-YOURSELF GAGS

STARTLING CONTRAPTIONS

JOY BUZZER

The classic Joy Buzzer gag is a circular metallic contraption that's hidden in your hand by a small loop that fits over your ring finger. You wind up the device, and when someone pushes the button by shaking your hand, the joy buzzer unwinds and vibrates a bit, "shocking" the person who was foolish enough to "shake on it."

It's a classic gag, but like many classic gags, it's not that good.

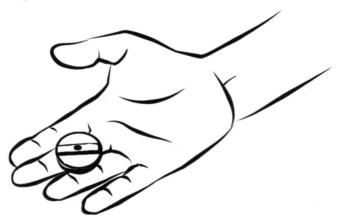

This is an updated version of the Joy Buzzer called the Super Sparker. This is an ordinary disposable camera that lets out an incredibly loud spark, causing the person who is nearest the camera to wet their pants in fright. Get an adult to help you with this project, because that's the person you're going to prank.

The secret to the Super Sparker is an electronic component called a capacitor. Capacitors are kind of like electronic water balloons; they can hold a lot of electricity, but when a metal object touches both wire leads, they "pop" all their electricity at once, releasing a powerful and disturbing spark.

ALWAYS BE CAREFUL

This prank involves serious electricity, enough to cause burns! Do not use the Super Sparker on small children, or anyone with a heart condition. Always use an insulated screwdriver, and above all, do not touch the capacitor with your bare hands!

How to Build the Super Sparker:

You will need:	
• Disposable camera	• The Internet
• Insulated screwdriver (rubber or plastic handle)	

Money required:		Time required:	
About $10.00		1 hour	
Success rate:	65 percent	Mischief level:	9

1. Disposable cameras have a rechargeable flash, which is connected to a powerful capacitor. If you want to be sure your disposable camera has enough "juice" for the Super Sparker, then buy a new one (they cost

about ten dollars). But since you're just going to be taking it apart anyway, you can try asking at your local drugstore for a couple of empty disposable camera cases (they usually have some behind the photo counter). Try to get a few, just in case the first one doesn't work. If they ask why, tell them you're building a ham radio.

2 Before you open the camera case, you must discharge (or "pop") the flash capacitor. This is a 300 volt capacitor that can cause painful electric shocks, and leave burns on your skin. Be careful! To discharge, press the shutter button and advance the film in the camera if needed. If the camera doesn't flash, you should proceed very carefully, as the capacitor may already be fully charged. (Or the battery may be dead.)

3 Peel off any stickers on the camera and gently crack open the case. Since these cameras are meant to be opened, you shouldn't have to use much force; just pull off the back, where you'll find an electronics board featuring a battery, flashbulb, and a large cylinder-shaped capacitor. Do not touch the capacitor.

4 Now you will test the spark, so get ready. Using an insulated screwdriver (with a rubber or plastic handle), touch the blade of the screwdriver to both capacitor wires. This "shorts" the capacitor by creating a path for the stored electricity to shoot over to the other side, draining the electricity and making an extremely loud

spark. When this happens, try not to wet your pants, as urine conducts electricity.

5 If the camera didn't spark (or didn't spark loudly enough), try again with another camera—your battery may be dead. If you did get a spark, advance the film in the camera (if needed) and press the flash recharge button to load up the capacitor again. Give it a few minutes to fully charge, and your prank will be ready to go.

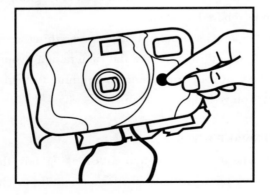

6 Go to www.mischiefmakersmanual.com/tools/sparker/ and print out the fake "instructions" there. This will fool your adult into thinking they are following harmless instructions for turning a disposable camera into a digital camera, which is possibly the silliest idea ever. The hardest part will be keeping a straight face as you present the instructions to them.

7 Find an adult you want to prank (parent, science teacher, study hall monitor, etc.) Bring over the camera, the screwdriver, and the fake instructions, being careful not to touch the capacitor. Ask if they'll help you, and point to the appropriate step on the fake instructions.

8 When the moment of the Super Spark occurs, be sure to let out a very loud, surprised yell, which will make the fright that much greater for your adult. If possible, drop a heavy tool on the table at the same time. If you have a friend nearby, get him/her to yell, too. Afterward, it's okay to laugh—just pretend that you're laughing because you're relieved to be alive.

9 Say "I guess we shouldn't believe everything we read on the Internet!" as you take the camera away, your hands shaking. If your adult wants to continue to help, simply say, "You've helped enough."

RATTLESNAKE EGGS

The classic gag is an authentic-looking box that says "Rattlesnake Eggs." It looks like it's a scientific specimen of some sort, but when you lift the lid, a paper clip tightly wound around a rubber band "rattles" wildly, imitating the sound of a rattlesnake. It doesn't really sound like a rattlesnake, but it is slightly startling.

The contraption is easy enough to rig yourself using common desk supplies, and with a little imagination it can be used in a variety of places:

- An envelope that reads "DO NOT OPEN"
- A carton of real eggs
- An Altoids tin

To make Rattlesnake Eggs, find the eggs of a rattlesnake, crack them into a pan, and cook over low flame with butter and a little oil. Only kidding. Here are the real instructions:

How to Make Rattlesnake Eggs:

You will need:	
• Envelope (or other container) • Sturdy rubber band • Small paper clip	• Small piece of sturdy wire (large paper clip or wire coat hanger)
Money required:	**Time required:**
Free	30 minutes
Success rate: 75 percent	**Mischief level:** 2

1. Bend the piece of sturdy wire until it looks something like this. This is your "holder" for the rubber band.

2. String the rubber band across the wire until it looks

something like this. It should be fairly tight, but not in danger of breaking.

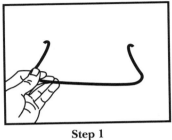

Step 1

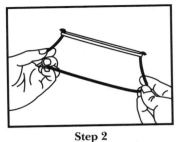

Step 2

3 String the paper clip across the rubber band like this.

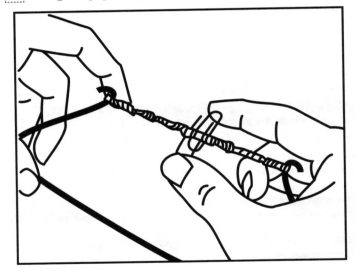

4 Wind the paper clip until it is tight, but not in danger of breaking. Be careful not to let go, as a furiously wound paper clip can really sting.

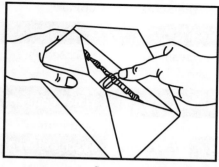

Step 4

5 Carefully put the prank in your envelope, egg carton, or other container. When you close it, the contraption should not go off—if it does, take it out and **tweak** as necessary until the gag works correctly.

> **Tweak:** To adjust or fine-tune something. *"I can't go to the movies, I've got to stay in and tweak this cow-pie launcher."* Can also be used as a noun: "Tweaks" are small incremental improvements.

SCREAMING CABINET

Every time you go to the drugstore or Wal-Mart, look for those musical greeting cards that play a little song when they're opened. These are perfect for all kinds of pranks. The more startling the sound, the better. Sometimes around Halloween you can find screaming or moaning sound chips, which are best of all.

How to Make the Screaming Cabinet:

You will need:	
• Musical or screaming greeting card	• Scissors • Tape

Money required:	Time required:
Free	30 minutes

Success rate:	75 percent	Mischief level:	3

1. Open the card and observe the sound chip closely. Notice how it is attached to the two sides of the card. Sometimes the chips have a speaker and wires attached; sometimes they're all in one piece.

2. Now look for the little flap or switch that "breaks" the electrical circuit when you open or close the card. When metal is no longer touching metal, the circuit is "open" or off. It is often a small piece of plastic that slides in and out as you open and close the card.

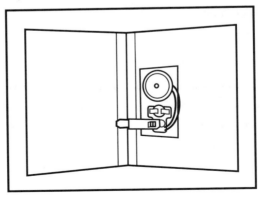

3 Using scissors, carefully cut away all the card until you only have the sound chip apparatus, the speaker, and a flap on each side. Make the flaps big enough that you'll have plenty of surface area to tape. It should look like a mini version of your original card.

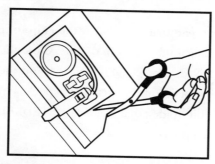

4 Using plenty of tape, attach the sound chip to the inside of the cabinet. Do not tape the other side of the card to the other side of the cabinet, because the card needs to be closed more than 90 degrees. Instead, put some extra circles of tape on the outside, or improvise something for use as a spacer. Tape is your friend.

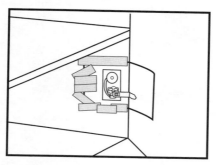

DO-IT-YOURSELF GAGS

5 Test and tweak.

6 Close the cabinet. The nice thing about this prank is that it's just "set it and forget it." You don't have to stick around and watch what happens; you can just go about your business. When it works, you'll hear it.

Another great idea is to attach the chip to the inside of a large folder, again using a ton o' tape. Close the folder and write "PERSONAL" or "CONFIDENTIAL" on the front. The idea is to trick people into sneaking a peek. Put a piece of paper inside the folder that reads "BUSTED!" Try to find a sound chip of a police siren.

WATER DEVICES

THE PERFECT WATER BALLOON

The beauty of a water balloon is its simplicity. Don't try to improve on the two classic ingredients: **balloons** and **water**. Contemplate, young prankster, on how two simple ingredients can be transformed into a hilarious, clothes-drenching prank.

You may be tempted to fill the balloons with something other than water. The problem with mustard balloons, ketchup balloons, relish balloons, syrup balloons, applesauce balloons, and Jell-O balloons is that they present a mess to be cleaned up. Pudding balloons can be funny when dropped from a blimp, but that's about it.

With a water balloon, there's not much they can make you do, with the exception of making you clean up the shreds of broken balloon, which only takes five minutes. *It's just water!*

An effective water balloon can be improvised with nearly any water source and any type of balloon. Balloons can be purchased at most drugstores and grocery stores, although party supply stores or the Internet have the greatest selection.

Match the size of the water balloon to the prank. Generally speaking, smaller balloons (about the size of a large orange) are ideal for throwing speed and maximum velocity. Larger balloons, on the other hand, make a satisfying splash when dropped from a rooftop or high window.

One of the most hilarious ways of launching is by using the **M3 Power Launcher**, which you can build yourself for about thirty dollars (see page 155). Match the size of your balloon to the size of the funnel. When using high-powered slingshots like the M3PL, be sure to aim it away from people, car windshields, or low-flying aircraft.

DON'T DAMAGE, DEFACE, OR DESTROY

With all water- and liquid-based pranks, following a few important rules will greatly decrease your chances of getting in trouble:

1. Don't use any liquid that would leave stains (Kool-Aid, Hawaiian Punch, anything with food coloring, etc.).
2. Do not freeze water balloons, or fill with anything heavy. **Always Be Careful** (page 23).
3. The best time to execute water-based mischief is during the hot summer months, when people are already wearing light clothes that are easy to change. The ideal location for water-balloon mischief is a pool, because nobody can get too mad about it.

How to Make a Ton of Water Balloons:

You will need:	
• Water balloons • Water source	• Ice chest, cooler, or other container
Money required:	**Time required:**
Varies	Varies
Success rate: 100 percent	**Mischief level:** 2

1 This is a two-person operation. First, have a trusted partner fit the balloon over the faucet.

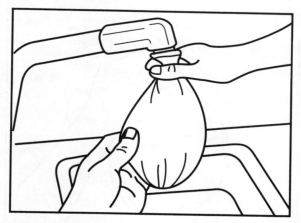

2 Turn on the water source, until balloon is *almost* filled. **DO NOT OVERFILL.** Leaving an inch or two at the top will make it easier to tie. Turn off the water source.

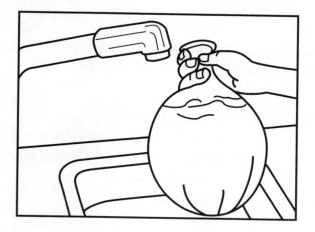

3 Have your partner pinch shut the balloon at the point where it is filled, giving you plenty of rubber for knotting.

4 Tie a perfect Balloon Knot (see **Figure 1**), while your partner begins repeating Step 1.

By using the methods on the previous pages, you will form an **assembly line**, capable of churning out fifty water balloons an hour, or more.

Assembly line: A system in a factory that produces many units of a particular item (like water balloons). Assembly lines should also be used for large-scale pranks like **The Post-It Note Makeover** (page 196). It is your job to organize these.

FIGURE 1: THE BALLOON KNOT

Some novices have difficulty tying the knot in the balloon. Practice, young prankster, until the knot-tying motion comes as naturally as breathing.

1. With one hand pinching the neck of the water balloon shut, stick out your first two fingers.

2. Wrap the neck of the balloon around your fingers, like a principal chasing a prankster.

3. The prankster escapes through the hole between the two fingers.

4. Pull to tighten.

DO-IT-YOURSELF GAGS

A third person can be added to collect the water balloons, and store them in a pail, cooler, or a large plastic organizing container. Be warned that the container will grow very heavy, so think carefully about your base location (each gallon of water weighs 8.34 pounds). Don't leave balloons in the hot sun; cover them, or leave them in a cool location.

Depending on the size of your mischief team, you can multiply this two- or three-person operation to multiple water sources, which can massively increase production. The largest water-balloon battle on record was held in Sydney, Australia, with over 50,000 water balloons. How do you think they filled up all those balloons? One at a time.

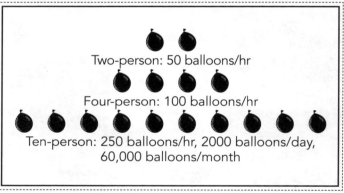

Two-person: 50 balloons/hr

Four-person: 100 balloons/hr

Ten-person: 250 balloons/hr, 2000 balloons/day, 60,000 balloons/month

✓ Practice tying ten water balloons. Take them into your yard and hurl them.

DISHTIME DRENCHER

This is a classic prank where you **rig** a kitchen sink hand-sprayer so that when someone turns on the main faucet, they get a full-on spray of water to the chest. Dishtime Drencher is a classic prank to pull in the kitchen at your summer camp or vacation home.

It only works on hand-sprayers that have a handle that can be pushed down. You use several rubber bands (or clear tape) to hold the button onto the handle. The idea is that the sprayer is always in the "ON" position, and you can use the holder to aim the spray where you want it to go.

The funniest place to aim the spray is the crotch, because it makes them look like they wet their pants. This is a high-risk move, however, as you're likely to hit the floor, or the inside of the sink. The holder can be rigged to point anywhere, although squirting in the face (called a "Wethead") is likely to make them angry.

DO-IT-YOURSELF GAGS

> **Rig:** To manipulate physical items in a mischievous way (e.g., **rigging a drawer** to make a loud bang when opened).

How to Rig a Hand-Sprayer:

You will need:	
• Rubber bands	• Hand-sprayer
Money required:	**Time required:**
Free	A few minutes
Success rate: 90 percent	**Mischief level:** 1

1. Take several sturdy rubber bands, and fit them over the head of a kitchen hand-sprayer, so the spray button is pressed down.

2. Test by pointing into the sink and turning on the water.

3. Replace the hand-sprayer in its holder so that it points directly at you.

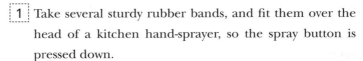

✓ Make sure you are stocked up on rubber bands, which come in handy for a wide array of mischief.

WWW.MISCHIEFMAKERSMANUAL.COM

DRIBBLE GLASS

The idea behind the classic Dribble Glass prank is that when someone goes to take a drink of their beverage, it "dribbles" down their arm through a series of small cuts or holes hidden in the cup. You can use your Swiss Army knife to carefully make slits—or a funnier method is to use a hole punch (see instructions on next page).

The best strategy for executing the Dribble Glass is to find a gathering where large groups of people are eating (large picnic, wedding, funeral). At a convenient time before the meal is served, rig the Dribble Glasses in another location, then replace them in their original location. If you pull this off without getting caught, someone else will serve the Dribble Glass, which keeps the attention off you.

The Dribble Glass gag below works on plastic or paper

cups that have a strong dark pattern or design (stripes, cartoon characters, etc.).

How to Make the Dribble Glass:

You will need:	
• Paper or plastic cups with loud, busy patterns	• Hole punch
Money required:	**Time required:**
Free	30 minutes
Success rate: 30 percent	**Mischief level:** 3

1 Borrow the cups, and take them to another location.

2 Using a hole punch, punch two to four holes in the pattern, near the top of the cup. Try to make it look like part of the pattern, if possible. Make the punches at evenly spaced points on the cup.

3 Repeat for about half the cups in the stack. Doing this with a partner and an extra hole punch makes it go faster.

Be sure to collect the little punched-out bits and throw them away in a secret trash can.

4 | Put the cups back on top of the bag or container, or mix them around randomly, and replace the cups where you found them.

5 | Serve and enjoy!

☑ Make a Dribble Glass. Experiment with your holes or slits for maximum dribbling effect.

BODILY NOISES

SNEEZING POWDER

One of the patron saints of pranking was a brilliant man by the name of S.S. Adams, who invented the original versions of many of the classic pranks featured in this book: Dribble Glass (page 138), Joy Buzzer (page 120), Snake in the Nuts (page 166), and the prank that started him off: **Cachoo Sneezing Powder**.

Soren Sorenson Adams, or "Sam" to his friends, was working as a salesman for a coal company in 1904, when he discovered a coal-tar powder that made people *sneeze like freaking crazy*. This mysterious powder had a sneeze factor, or "sneezosity," much greater than pepper. Eureka! A prank was born.

There are stories of S.S. blowing his patented sneezing powder into a crowded room of business executives, who would erupt into massive sneezing fits. (He probably didn't get many promotions.) Or he would blow sneezing powder into a brass band as they walked by, and the band would have to stop the parade in order to sneeze watery mucus from their eyes and noses.

Why would a man ever think he could build a company on *sneezing powder*? That question remains a mystery, but S.S. quit his job and set up the Cachoo Sneezing Powder company. If he hadn't taken that mad, crazy gamble, you wouldn't be reading these words today.

Wacky little Cachoo became a national fad. There are stories of churches, classrooms, and entire sports teams pranked by Cachoo. Realizing he had a hit on his hands, S.S. Adams changed the name of his company to "S.S. Adams," to show he was not a one-product company. Then he began to make breakthrough after incredible breakthrough. The Squirting Cigarette Lighter. The Bleeding Finger. The Squirting Nickel. The Stink Bomb. The Exploding Package. The guy was a genius. He was the Thomas Edison of troublemaking.

So: *What was in Cachoo?* S.S. never revealed his secret formula, but scholars now believe it was a chemical called *dianisidine*, which was later found to cause cancer. Today you can still buy "sneezing powder" off the Internet, but it usually contains nothing but finely ground black pepper, which you can easily make yourself.

How to Make Sneezing Powder:

You will need:	
• Freshly ground pepper (from a pepper mill)	• Mortar and pestle • Spoon
Money required:	**Time required:**
Free	15 minutes
Success rate: 90 percent	**Mischief level:** 1

1. Take a pepper grinder and grind one tablespoon (or more) of black pepper. You need fresh-ground pepper, not regular pepper that comes in cans or shakers.

2 Using a mortar and pestle, grind the pepper down until it is a fine powder.

3 Put it in a big spoon and hold it under someone's nose, asking, "Do these spices smell fresh to you?"

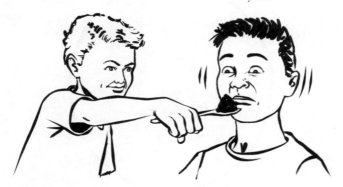

This makes some people sneeze, some get burning mucous membranes, and some get red and irritated. A few are immune to black pepper altogether, but dianisidine is illegal, so this is the best you've got. Give pepper a chance.

WHOOPEE CUSHIONS

The modern-day Whoopee Cushion (also known as Poo-Poo Cushion, or Razzberry Cushion if you live in England) was invented in 1950 by employees at the Jem Rubber Company of Toronto, Canada, who were goofing around with scrap sheets of rubber in the workshop. They glued two halves of rubber together, leaving a balloonlike nozzle on the end. To their endless delight, they discovered that filling it with air, then sitting on it, made a sound like a butt bugle.

FIGURE 1: THE ORIGINAL

Figure 1 shows the package of an early **Razzberry Cushion**, featuring an illustration of an opera lady sitting down on the device, which makes the surprising sound *BRA-A-ACK!* (It's difficult to spell the noise a fart makes.)

FIVE FUNNY WHOOPEE-CUSHION RESPONSES:

- "Who cut the cheese without passing the crackers?"
- "We've got to get that oiled."
- "Someone call the gas company. We've got a leak."
- "Nice one, Sir Stinkalot." ("Madam Mudbaby" may be used for girls.)
- "Somebody just cut a party platter of cheese."

FIGURE 2: THE CLASSIC

Figure 2 is the **Classic Whoopee Cushion** that everyone remembers today. "When anyone sits down, it emits a REAL Bronx cheer," reads the caption. ("Bronx cheer" was slang for "blowing a raspberry.") In this illustration, the whoopee cushion makes the sound *POO!* as the victim sits on it, which was a big improvement over *BRA-A-ACK!*, probably the result of years of whoopee cushion consumer research.

PROS: CHEAP, HILARIOUS
CONS: EASY TO BREAK, DIFFICULT TO HIDE

FIGURE 3: THE SELF-INFLATOR

Figure 3 shows the next innovation in pooting technology, the **Self-Inflator**. Self-inflators work by using a springy foam that draws air into the device automatically, which saves you the trouble of trying to get the little rubber nozzle open to blow into it (they tend to stick). Self-inflators produce a slightly different sound than the Classic, with a muffled flatulence that sounds like somebody tore open a hot, juicy breakfast biscuit.

PROS: SMALLER, EASIER TO OPERATE
CONS: STILL REQUIRES A DIRECT BUTT HIT

FIGURE 4: THE ELECTRONIC POOTER

Figure 4 shows **The Electronic Pooter,** an extremely hilarious modern version of the Whoopee Cushion. This is a remote-control fart machine that you set behind someone's chair. You hide the remote control in your pocket, and wait. At the perfect time, you secretly press a button in your pocket, and the machine lets 'er rip. It is virtually fail-safe, and wildly comical. Some of these machines have different trouser tones, and a few even come with a self-timer, which professionals call the "tooter timer."

PROS: EASY TO HIDE, RELIABLE
CONS: MORE EXPENSIVE, REQUIRES BATTERIES

Electronic Pooters are definitely the "crème de la crème" of farting machines, offering the power and control of the exact moment of the prank. Regardless, *some type* of gas-crack contraption should be in every good mischief maker's arsenal. For those who don't want to save up for the high-quality farting experience, a cheaper do-it-yourself option is available: the iPooter.

> ☑ Be able to explain to a partner the four types of whoopee cushions.
>
> WWW.MISCHIEFMAKERSMANUAL.COM

THE iPOOTER

The iPooter is the latest in AF (artificial flatulence) technology. It can be placed underneath a couch, desk, or church pew to let loose an unexpected trouser tuba. You can have it say random words like "Rutabaga," or you can do an occasional heavy grunt every five minutes. You can have a time-delayed fart that plays forty-five minutes into the future, during a conversation, meal, or service.

The wonderful thing about the iPooter is its versatility: It's only limited by your imagination. You can change the sound to a meowing cat, or you can "throw your voice" by leaving it in a foot locker. This handy little prank can be left in a quiet study hall, a car trunk, or anywhere it would be funny or unusual to hear someone's voice. Don't put it down a well. That freaks people out.

Possibly the most hilarious use of the iPooter is to record someone's name being called quietly, then hide it, or lower it in front of an open window where they're sitting. This prank will reduce anyone to quiet hysterics—the person who's madly trying to find the sound of the voice, and the person shaking with laughter on the other side.

How to Build the iPooter:

You will need:	
• iPod • Small battery-operated speakers	• Twine, cord, or heavy string
Money required:	Time required:
Less than $30.00 (if you own the iPod)	One hour
Success rate: 90 percent	Mischief level: 6

Assuming you own an iPod, the only expensive thing about the iPooter is the speakers. These should be battery-operated, and reasonably small. You could build the iPooter with a set of $3,000 stereo speakers, but you wouldn't want to lower those babies from a window.

The best part is, your family may already have battery-operated speakers somewhere in the house. If not, cheap speakers can be easily purchased at RadioShack, Wal-Mart, or eBay. "With these speakers, we'll be able to listen to your favorite music in the kitchen," is a convincing argument for most adults.

1 Download an appropriate prank MP3 file to your iPod: farts, delayed farts, bird calls, barking seals, crying babies, grunting, moaning, or vomiting. You can also record your own sound effects by using your school's audio lab or your home computer. Some MP3 players have voice-record features built in, which is like hitting the jack*poot*.

2 Take the iPod and the speakers and fit them together like this.

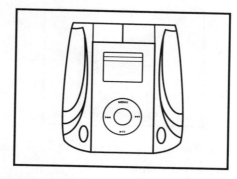

3 With your string or twine, wrap the entire bundle, again and again, in all directions, until everything is bound together firmly. For lightweight string, this may take an entire roll. Make sure the controls to the iPod remain showing.

4 Make a loop of string or twine on the top of the iPooter. This will operate not only as a handle to quickly move it from location to location, but also a hook for lowering the iPooter in front of a window.

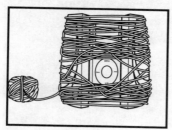

Step 3   **Step 4**

5 [Optional] If you want to finish it off, put clear tape around the handle.

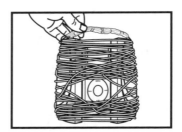

6 [Optional] Tie a rope or cord around the handle, depending on the prank.

IMPROVISING AN iPOOTER

- If you don't have a ball of string or twine handy, you can improvise many other things to tie together your iPooter (bungee cords, belts, shoelaces, large rubber bands, etc.). **Be creative**. Avoid tape, which can leave sticky residue on your speakers.
- You can also put the iPod and speakers in a pillowcase, and tie it securely with a rope or cord, although this makes it more difficult to access the iPod.
- If your family has the type of iPod speakers that plug into the wall, you can just hide the iPod and speakers behind a desk or couch, making sure they're plugged into a hidden wall outlet. Use an extension cord if necessary. Although it's not portable, it can still be wildly hilarious as a one-time prank.

PROJECTILES

SLINGSHOTS

For centuries, slingshots have been the symbol of mischief makers the world over. In the biblical story of David versus Goliath, a young troublemaker named David kills the mighty Philistine giant Goliath, using nothing more than a slingshot and a couple of rocks.

David probably used an ancient **sling** (see **Figure 1**), which consisted of two long cords and a pouch to hold the ammo. The two cords were twirled over the head, then *one* line was released, using centrifugal force to hurl the rock with great speed—enough speed to *kill a twelve-foot fighting warrior.*

KA-THWOCK!

Figure 1: *Ancient Slingshot*

After stunning Goliath with the Slingshot of Death, David seized the sword of the giant and killed him, then cut off his head. (It's in the Bible; look it up.) Then he lifted up Goliath's head, dripping blood and neck tissue, and screamed. Not a girly scream, either, but a *warrior's scream.* The Philistine armies ran in fear, the Israelites let out a tremendous battle cry, and chased the Philistines back home to Outer Philistia.

All this because of a slingshot.

> ## ALWAYS BE CAREFUL
> Don't be like David: Never launch a slingshot at another person. Ever. That includes a person driving a car, or a school bus, or an airplane. Launch slingshots into empty fields, or off parking decks. Be safe, and please, for the love of Goliath, *use common sense.*

You can still find slings today, but modern mischief makers use a **slingshot** (see **Figure 2**) because of its portability and style. The modern slingshot is made of three materials: a Y-shaped stick or bar, a pouch or holder, and rubber bands or bungee cords. A quick slingshot can be improvised almost anywhere with these three basic ingredients.

You operate the slingshot by holding it in the hand you *don't write with.* Put your ammo in the pouch, hold the slingshot out in front of you, pull the pouch back with your opposite hand as far as you dare, and release.

PA-THOING!

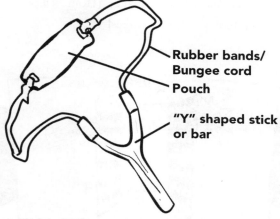

**Rubber bands/
Bungee cord**

Pouch

**"Y" shaped stick
or bar**

Figure 2: *Modern Slingshot*

Professional mischief makers want something with a little
more slinging power: the **M3 Power Launcher.** It is an *extremely
powerful* slingshot that can be used to launch water balloons,
pieces of fruit, or frogs. It consists of two bungee cords tied
between two large trees, with a plastic funnel for the "pouch."
Best of all, the M3PL can be made for less than thirty dollars.

How to Build the M3 Power Launcher:

You will need:	
• Large funnel	• Water balloons
• 30 feet of rubber tubing	

Money required:		Time required:	
Less than $30.00		One hour	
Success rate:	90 percent	**Mischief level:**	6

1 Go to your local home retailer (Home Depot, Lowe's, etc.) and look for the funnel aisle.

2 Find a plastic funnel that's large enough to hold a water balloon about the size of an apple. Find a store employee and ask to have four holes drilled in the side of the large funnel. If they ask why, tell them you're making a robot costume.

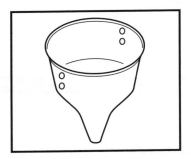

3 Buy the rest of the materials, and head home.

4 Cut the rubber tubing in half.

5 Thread each half through the holes, so you have four rubber ends dangling freely.

6 Tie the funnel around a pair of trees, fence posts, or football field goals.

7 Load, aim, and fire!

CATAPULTS

Catapults are complicated machines that use physics and math to hurl objects (like physics and math books) at great distances. Originally used as ancient weapons of war, three-ton wheeled catapults hurled mighty boulders into castle walls and had to be pushed forward by an army of men.

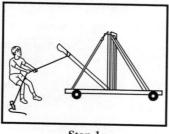

Step 1

Step 2

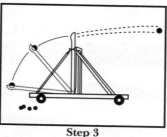

Step 3

Nowadays, it is difficult to find castles, unless you live in an upscale neighborhood. But people still make catapults. Sometimes they're as small as **mini catapults** made out of toothpicks and rubber bands, and sometimes they're as powerful as the **ACME Catapult**, a "monster catapult" machine built by a bunch of guys in Illinois. It can hurl refrigerators, lawn tractors, or a washing machine high into the air. (This thing has to be seen to be believed—Google "acme catapult video" to see it in action.)

You can build a powerful catapult capable of hurling eggs, tennis balls, tomatoes, and other round objects. The advantage of a catapult over the M3 Power Launcher is that it's much better for places where you can't tie the M3PL. The secret to building a catapult is to buy a **catapult kit**, which has all the wood, ropes, screws, and other materials you need to build a real, working catapult.

Although the price varies (you can spend hundreds of dollars on huge catapults), a decent working catapult can be bought for under thirty dollars. And there's an easy way to get a catapult kit *for free*. Get an adult to buy it for you.

How to Get Your Parents to Buy You a Catapult:

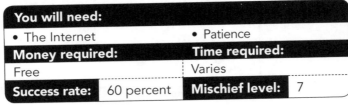

You will need:			
• The Internet		• Patience	
Money required:		Time required:	
Free		Varies	
Success rate:	60 percent	Mischief level:	7

1. Google "catapult kit" for a wide selection of ready-to-assemble catapults. When you've found the catapult kit you want, bookmark the page to give your parents the hint.

2. At the dinner table, ask your parents what an engineer does for a living (not a *train* engineer, but a *mechanical* engineer). Announce that you're learning about engineers at school, and say you're thinking about becoming an engineer. Then drop the subject.

3. A few days later, ask your parents, "What's physics?" Your parents won't have a good answer for this one, but pretend to remain politely interested as they struggle for a response. If they ask why you're interested, remind them you want to be an engineer.

4. Then a few days later, bring up the subject of catapult kits. Say you found them while you were researching physics on the Internet. Ask if they'll buy one for you. If the answer is no, accept this calmly, and mention that a catapult kit might make a good birthday present.

5. Continue to bring up the subject of catapult kits, once every three days, until your parents finally give in. Your argument should go something like this: "The world needs good engineers, and the kids who want to be engineers need a way to get hands-on experience with physics and engineering." This is the truth. They won't be able to argue with this.

6. Congratulations! You closed the sale. The hard part is

over. Once you get your catapult in the mail, most catapult kits can be built in a day. Fire and enjoy!

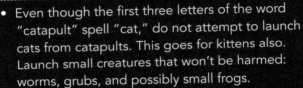

ALWAYS BE CAREFUL

- Even though the first three letters of the word "catapult" spell "cat," do not attempt to launch cats from catapults. This goes for kittens also. Launch small creatures that won't be harmed: worms, grubs, and possibly small frogs.
- Similarly, never *aim* a catapult at any living thing, with the exception of large trees. Fire into an empty area, like a field or river.
- If you're firing anything like yogurt or Jell-O containers, be sure to clean up the plastic containers or other trash. Ordinary food can usually be left behind for animals to enjoy.
- Use common sense. Always check catapult parts for wear before firing. If they look like they might break, be sure to replace them before using. Treat the catapult with respect. Otherwise: YOU'LL SHOOT YOUR EYE OUT!

FROGS RAINING FROM THE SKIES

The frog, like the slingshot, has long been a calling card of professional mischief makers. The frog is a harmless creature that is still very surprising to find in your soup, your bathtub, your car, your toilet, your bed, your nightstand, your shirt, your underwear, your hat, your hair, or hurling through the air at twenty to thirty miles per hour.

TOAD TRAPPING TIPS

- Frogs and toads are certain to jump away from you, so make sure they won't escape somewhere you can't get them (like into a bush). Try to corner the frog so it's near a yard or open field.
- To catch a toad, just grab it as quickly as you can, with two hands. It will be cold, wet, and slimy, but you must resist the urge to let go. Do not squeeze so tightly that you injure the frog.
- If the frog leaps out of your hands, calmly chase it back down and grab it again. Do not panic. Humans are quicker than frogs.
- Always wash your hands after handling frogs to remove bacteria and slimy frog goo.

Many people are freaked out by frogs, due to their weird appearance and slimy disposition. They were one of the plagues of Moses, and many people think they cause warts (not true, of course; only human viruses cause warts). The most harm a frog can do is urinate on your hands, which they do frequently, so try not to release them in fright when this happens.

The best place to find frogs is a pond, stream, or other body of water. You can often put out a large container of water in a wooded area (like a clean trash-can lid), leave it for a few days, and frogs will find it.

Because launching live frogs from slingshots or catapults can injure the frog (small frogs are usually okay, as long as they are fired into a pond or body of water), a better way is to launch a **dead frog**, which can easily be purchased off the Internet for a few dollars.

How to Make Frogs Rain from the Skies:

You will need:	
• The Internet	• An M3 Power Launcher or catapult
Money required:	**Time required:**
Less than $15.00	A few days
Success rate: 90 percent	**Mischief level:** 7

1. Google "frog dissection kit" to find companies that sell frog dissection kits for high school biology classes. These companies usually have a wonderful assortment of disgusting items: dead frogs, cow eyes, sheep brains, foot-long earthworms, and other assorted animal organs. Usually these are preserved in chemicals, which means they don't need to be refrigerated; you can store them in your closet or basement until you need them.

2. Build one of the catapults or slingshots featured in this section. If it's powerful enough to launch a water balloon, it's powerful enough to launch a frog.

3. Load up your frog, aim, and fire. The great part about using a dead frog is that you can launch it against the side of a building, tree, or sturdy metal sign. Don't let adults catch you doing this, or they will probably send you to counseling.

SURPRISE FOOD

THE BUG IN THE ICE CUBE

This is the classic "Bug in the Ice Cube" gag, which costs either a few dollars, or 200,000 Skee-Ball tickets (see **Figure 1**). The idea is that you drop it into someone's iced beverage, hoping they'll notice it, freak out, then drop the drink in their lap.

It rarely works out that way. Most bug gags are made of cheap plastic, and do not look very believable, which is why you should follow these plans for a *homemade* bug in an ice cube. This version of the gag will have much greater odds of success, since it uses a *real bug*.

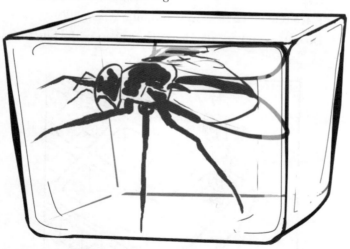

Figure 1: *The Bug in the Ice Cube*

How to Make the Bug in the Ice Cube:

You will need:	
• The Internet • Dead bug • Water	• Light-colored beverage (lemonade, Sprite, water, etc.)
Money required:	**Time required:**
Free	Several hours
Success rate: 75 percent	**Mischief level:** 2

1 Find a dead bug. The best bugs are dead worms, which are easy to find on the sidewalk after it rains. Using more than one worm makes them easier to see.

2 Rinse bug under running water. The last thing you need is someone to get sick from an improperly washed worm.

3 Place bug in ice cube tray, and fill tray *half-full* with water. Do not overfill. Smaller ice cubes will make the bug easier to spot.

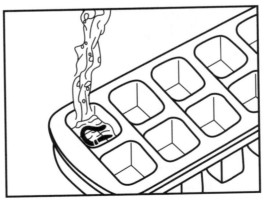

4 Freeze for approximately four hours, then remove cubes from tray. They will look like this.

5 Stack cubes in clear drinking glass. Use only two or three ice cubes, with wormy ice on top. Pour beverage over ice, and serve.

166

SNAKE IN THE NUTS

This prank should actually be called "Spiders in the Pringles," but it is named "Snake in the Nuts" in honor of the original prank, a container of mixed nuts that, when opened, pops out a coiled "snake." It's just that "Snake in the Nuts" is a funnier name.

The version you'll learn below is more effective, because it uses a modern snack tube (like Pringles) to lure them in. When they take off the lid to grab a handful of delicious, salty potato chips, out pop a *dozen surprising spiders instead*!

How to Put Spiders in the Pringles:

You will need:	
• Empty Pringles can • Freshness seal • Plastic cup • Two 9" rubber bands (or four 5" rubber bands)	• Black paper • Black yarn (optional) • Clear tape • Packing tape

Money required:		Time required:	
Free		One hour	
Success rate:	60 percent	Mischief level:	4

1 If the Pringles can has a transparent lid, you want to take

the "freshness seal" and stick it into the underside of the lid (use tape if necessary), so people can't see into the can.

2 Using your scissors, cut the bottom of the plastic cup to create a "plunging platform." Cut down the sides until you have only a quarter-inch lip around the bottom. Make sure the platform fits inside the can with plenty of room. You do not want a snug fit.

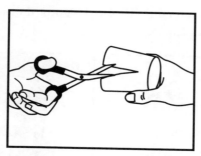

3 Cross two 9" rubber bands, making an *X*, and tape them to the bottom of the platform. (If you don't have 9" rubber bands, you can use four 5" rubber bands.) You should now have a platform with four long elastic loops.

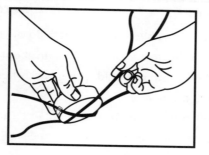

4 Punch four holes around the top of the Pringles can, just below the edge.

5 Thread the rubber bands from the inside of the can to the outside of the can, and tape them down on the inside. Tape all around the inside of the can, so you have a solid ring of tape.

6 Use small pieces of clear tape on the outside to hold down the 1/2" tails of rubber band around the top. Don't worry too much about these; the design of the can is so crazy that most people won't see them.

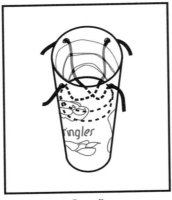

Step 5

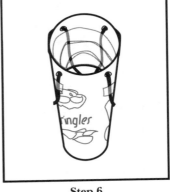

Step 6

7 With all four rubber bands taped down, the platform should now be floating inside the can, about three inches from the top, and it should spring back when you push it down with a spoon.

8 Next you must build the spiders. You can use plastic spiders, or you can take twelve sheets of black paper and wad each of them into small "pucks," about the size of Triple Stuf Oreo cookies. Wrap the spiders in clear packing tape. (The spiders need slick bodies, so they will slide along the inside of the can.)

9 Attach "legs" made of black yarn or paper. The spiders don't actually need to look that much like spiders, because they will be flying into someone's face.

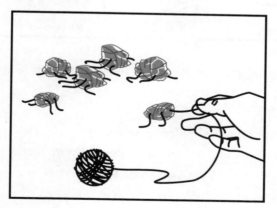

|10| Load the can by stacking the spiders on top of one another, one at a time. Push down the internal platform with more spiders, until the rubber bands are stretched and the can is trying to shoot them out. While holding the spiders down with one hand, slide the cover on with the other hand. It should hold them in.

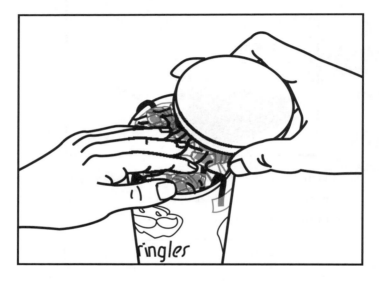

|11| Put the Pringles can where someone is likely to enjoy it. Be sure to have a video camera handy.

For even more spidery goodness, you may wish to put a short empty Coke can on top of the platform, then layer the spiders on top of the Coke can. This operates as a "spacer" that allows *all* the spiders to safely escape.

DIET COKE EXPLOSION

Every mischief maker knows that a Mentos candy dropped into a two-liter bottle of Diet Coke will result in the eruption of a *mighty soda geyser*. But only skilled troublemakers, who have studied the secret art of mischief, know how to rig the Diet Coke Explosion so it erupts on *someone else*.

How to Make the Diet Coke Explosion:

You will need:	
• 2-liter bottle of Diet Coke • Mentos	• Needle and thread • Hammer • Scissors
Money required:	**Time required:**
Less than $5.00	30 minutes
Success rate: 85 percent	**Mischief level:** 6

1 Lay the Mentos on a work surface. Place a needle in the center of the Mentos, and gently tap with a hammer until you can thread the needle through the other side. If the Mentos breaks, start again with another. It's only Mentos.

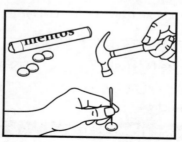

2 Tie the thread loosely to itself to secure the Mentos.

3 Open the Diet Coke. Hang the Mentos over the side, with the thread over the lip of the bottle.

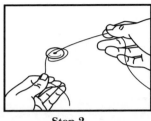

Step 2   **Step 3**

4 *Carefully* put the cap back on, and tighten. Perform this step over a sink, with the bottle pointing away from your face, just in case anything explodes.

5 Snip the end of the thread off, so the prank is invisible. When they screw off the top, the Mentos should now be poised to drop into the Diet Coke, causing a cold, brown, carbonated jet of chaos.

Regular Coke will also work, but it makes a sticky mess afterward. Diet Coke is better. Either way, you should offer to help clean up, while you vow to help them catch the person who did it.

☑ Practice the Diet Coke Explosion. Have your partner take it into the yard and open it, to make sure it was built correctly.

THE SCIENCE OF SPEWING SODA

Mentos have millions of microscopic nooks and crannies. These are called **nucleation sites**, places where bubbles of carbon dioxide can form. And Diet Coke is already full of carbon dioxide, just waiting to be released into gas (carbon dioxide gives Diet Coke its familiar fizz).

When you drop the candy into the Diet Coke, the Mentos loads up on carbon dioxide. The water in the Diet Coke "resists" this giant belch, and the resulting "power struggle" between water and CO_2 is what causes the mighty *blork!* of soda out the top.

You can see a similar effect, though not nearly as cool, when you drop a scoop of ice cream into root beer.

EXPLODING DEVICES

EXPLODING CIGARETTE

Cigarettes are bad for you. That's a medical fact. So if you know anyone who still smokes, an exploding cigarette is an "intervention" to help them stop. It's not a prank; it's a *public service*. After a few exploding cigarettes, the smoker will be fearful of lighting up.

The technical term for the device is a "cigarette load." Although they've been available in novelty catalogs for years, it's much easier to make one yourself, and as an added bonus you'll learn how to make a cheap homemade firecracker (see **Figure 1: Exploding Firecracker**).

WARNING: Smokers tend to get grumpy when they don't have their cigarettes. **This prank should be carried out with extreme caution**.

How to Pull off the Exploding Cigarette:

You will need:	
• A package of toy caps (the loud plastic kind that go in cap guns)	• Tiny square of tissue paper • Piece of paper • Sharp object
Money required:	**Time required:**
Less than $5.00	One hour
Success rate: 35 percent	**Mischief level:** 6

1 With your sharp instrument, poke a hole in each toy cap, and empty the powder onto a piece of paper. Clean out each cap thoroughly.

2 Using the paper as a funnel, collect the powder and put it into your square of tissue paper.

3 Make a little "pocket" out of the tissue paper, and twist the top closed. This is your cigarette load (see **Figure 1: Exploding Firecracker** for other ideas).

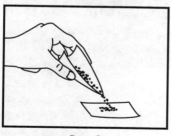

Step 2

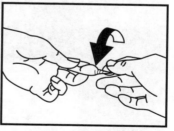

Step 3

4 Take the cigarette, and carefully scoop out tobacco from the end. The goal is to create a hole big enough to fit the cigarette load into.

5 Drop in the load and carefully replace tobacco in the end of the hole, so the load is invisible. Use extreme care when doing this step; be patient and start again with a fresh cigarette if necessary.

6 When the load is complete, put the cigarette back into the pack, and leave the pack where you found it. (This is the part that makes it really believable.)

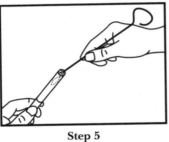 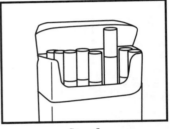

Step 5 **Step 6**

FIGURE 1: EXPLODING FIRECRACKER

Steps 1-3 can also be used to make a quickie homemade firecracker. To make a "fuse," simply roll masking tape until it resembles a long candlewick.

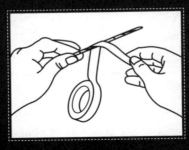

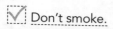
THE HAPPY CONFETTI GRENADE

This prank was made popular in the mid-1980s by Chinese schoolboys working in the electronics markets of Shanghai. The prank is a **film canister** that is placed or thrown into an unsuspecting area. After a few seconds: *KA-POW!* The film canister explodes in a shower of confetti.

Film canisters are used to hold 35mm camera film, still used by most non-digital cameras. This means film canisters are readily available at your local drugstore or anywhere you go to develop photos. Store employees will usually give you a couple for free if you ask nicely. Ask for the white or clear ones, which generally seal more tightly than the black ones.

Compressed air is usually used to blow dust out of computers. It's easily available at drugstores, Wal-Mart, etc. (Look in the computer section.)

The wonderful thing about the Happy Confetti Grenade is that it's *versatile*. It can be filled with many different things—not only the many different types of confetti (see **Five Types of Confetti**, page 178), but also substitutions like flour, baby powder, or even dried basil, if you want to make the room smell like lasagna. Or you can put nothing at all in the canister. The prank works so many different ways.

FIVE TYPES OF CONFETTI

Every mischief maker should be familiar with confetti, as it can be left in many convenient locations: under car visors, on top of ceiling fans, inside rolled-up projector screens. Here are five common types:

1. **Torn-up paper:** easy to improvise from a sheet of notebook paper; can be made anywhere.
2. **Cut-up paper:** takes a little more time, but worth it. If you have access to a paper cutter (available at Kinko's and in most art rooms), this goes even faster.
3. **Hole-punched paper:** maddeningly small, and beautifully symmetrical. Many hole punches have a little "confetti holder" that can be easily filled and emptied.
4. **Shredder confetti:** If you're lucky enough to have access to a crosscut paper shredder, it will pump out vast quantities of confetti in minutes.
5. **Store-bought confetti:** At party supply stores and drugstores, you can buy ready-made confetti that is often much fancier than you can make at home: shiny foil confetti in ridiculous shapes (party horns, Cupids, birthday cakes, etc.). When you want to impress someone with a prank, don't be afraid to splurge.

How to Make the Happy Confetti Grenade:

You will need:	
• 35mm film canister • Can of compressed air	• Piece of paper • Confetti

Money required:	Time required:
Less than $10.00	15 minutes

Success rate:	70 percent	Mischief level:	7

1 Turn the can of compressed air upside down, and spray it into the film canister. Do this gently and calmly, spraying the liquid down the side of the canister, which should be tilted at an angle. **WARNING:** The liquid that comes out is *extremely cold* and can cause severe burns! Keep away from skin.

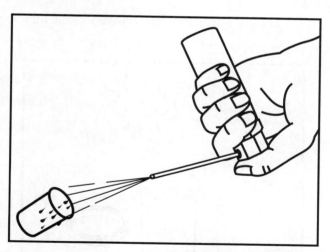

2 Quickly put your confetti inside the canister and close the lid. You need to have a tight seal on the lid for the pressure to build, so don't use too much confetti.

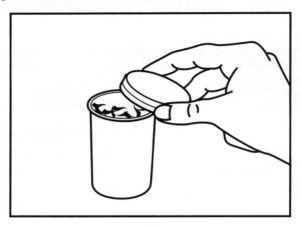

3 Quickly set down the canister, then get out of there. It will take anywhere from a few seconds to a full minute to explode. Stay away until it does.

THE EXPLOSION EXPLAINED

The "air" inside "compressed air" is our old friend carbon dioxide (CO_2), which is compressed into the can at high pressure. At high pressures, carbon dioxide turns into a liquid, which is what you hear when you shake the can.

By flipping the can upside down, it allows the liquid to escape into the canister. As the liquid warms inside the canister, it expands, eventually blowing the airtight lid off the top.

☑ Go to the photo-developing desk at a local store, and ask for a few film canisters. (They also come in handy for storing things.)

PURCHASING FIREWORKS IN THE UNITED STATES

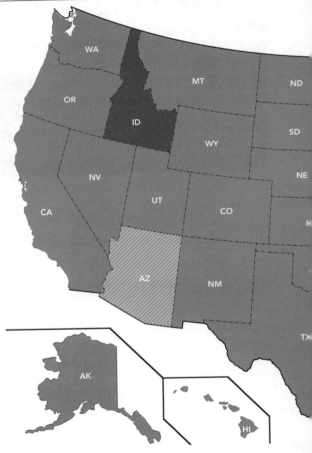

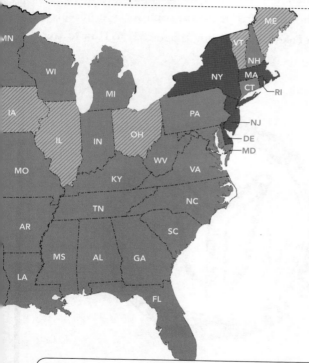

States that allow some or all types of consumer fireworks

States that only allow sparklers or other lame fireworks

States that do not allow any fireworks at all, which makes them unpatriotic

Look up your own state on the map, and memorize what types of fireworks are allowed.

PRANK RANK ACHIEVED!

Congratulations, young mischief maker. You have pranked hard, and learned well. You are now a **Major Mischief Maker**, and ready to be trained in the most sophisticated mischief, from **Staging a Fake UFO Landing** (page 232) to **How to Get on the Local News** (page 212).

Visit www.mischiefmakersmanual.com to track progress and download badge.

You are now only two levels away from achieving the ranking of **Master Mischief Maker**, your ultimate destiny. At this point, you are a legend in the making. Complete the next section, and your legend will be made.

EXPERTS ONLY

PRANKS WITH PARTNERS

WORLD'S LARGEST BUTT PHOTO

Every prankster should know how to create a *really* huge sign. This comes in handy for many pranks, like a ten-foot message wishing someone a happy birthday (when it's not really their birthday) or an enormous picture of a butt.

The **expensive** way is to go to Kinko's or a local print shop. Bring along your digital file, and ask them to turn it into a sign. They can print great-quality butt banners, but they'll charge you.

The **cheaper** way is to get access to a printer (fast laser printers work best) and a free online program called The Rasterbator (**www.mischiefmakersmanual.com/tools**

/rasterbator). This unfortunate name is a play on the word **rasterizing**, the process of turning an image into dots or smaller pieces (which is what it does). This site will accept any picture, and turn it into a file that you can easily print on regular pieces of 8.5 x 11" white paper (or colored paper, to give your sign a festive touch). You then trim the edges, and paste up all the pieces, one by one, until you form a giant photo collage. Also works for fake student council banners or ridiculous messages, but nothing beats a butt.

DON'T BE A BULLY

If you're going to use someone's photo, use this only on people who will be cool with it. Be prepared for a massive prank in return.

How to Create the World's Largest Butt Photo:

You will need:	
• Computer	• A partner
• Black-and-white printer (laser printer preferred)	• Time
• Paper cutter or scissors	• Patience

Money required:	Time required:
Free (if you can borrow the printer and paper)	A few days

Success rate:	50 percent	Mischief level:	7

1 Measure the wall. Decide how large you want your photo to be. (This prank is much easier if you measure no higher

than you or a partner can reach on a small stool; ladders
will slow you down.)

2 Prepare your digital image and upload it to www.
mischiefmakersmanual.com/tools/rasterbator. You can
also upload a photo from the Internet.

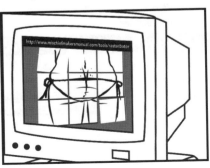

3 You will now have a PDF file that can be sent to any printer. Fast laser printers work best, but you can use an inkjet printer if you have enough ink refills ready.

4 Number each page in pencil on the reverse side, in case they get shuffled out of order.

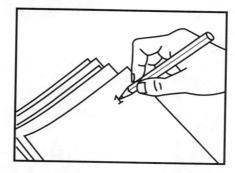

5 Trim off the white edges of each page. By far the fastest way to do this is with a paper cutter, which you'll find in most art classes, offices, and Kinko's. (Don't worry about getting every cut perfect.) You can use scissors if you're patient.

6. Pick a time and location where you'll have a good half hour to work uninterrupted. Post lookouts as needed.

7. With a partner, tape each page to the wall, one by one, moving left to right, top to bottom. After you complete each row, tape the corners of each page to the other corners. Use additional tape as necessary to secure. Don't be afraid of the tape.

8. Before you leave, be sure to get a picture of the picture. People will be talking about this prank for years to come. You want to make sure there's photo proof.

PHOTO TIPS

- **Use high-quality images.** The better quality the photo, the better quality the final prank.
- **Choose the smallest dot size available.** Choosing larger dot sizes will break it up into huge-dot patterns, which is useful if you just want to make cool artwork for your wall.
- **Change the file name.** Be forewarned, the program creates a file called rasterbation.pdf, which is not the kind of thing you want someone finding on your computer.

✓ Find your nearest source for a quality laser printer. This could be a library, school, a local print shop, or (if you're lucky) your home. See what the cost is, if any.

MY NEAREST LASER PRINTER IS:

_____

_____

_____

_____

_____

_____

_____

THE POST-IT NOTE MAKEOVER

Post-It Notes, those small sticky squares, were first introduced by the 3M Corporation in 1977, the invention of Dr. Spencer Silver (who had invented a glue that was only mildly sticky) and Art Fry (who had the idea to use the glue on pieces of paper). The product failed its first time out, but once the company convinced people to try the slightly sticky squares, everybody was hooked.

Now Post-It Notes (or similar "sticky notes") are everywhere, just waiting for mischief. They're perfect for quick signs or messages, where previous generations of pranksters had to use tape, or (in olden times) tree sap.

The Post-It Note Makeover is a large-scale stunt where you completely cover an object in Post-Its: a refrigerator, your mom's car, etc. If you have access to different colors of Post-Its, you can even make cool patterns—just sketch out your pattern first, using graph paper (see **Figure 1** and **Figure 2**).

Figure 1: *Plotting Your Post-Its*

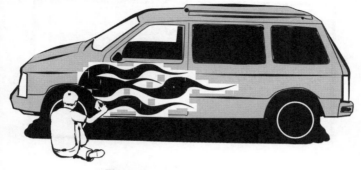

Figure 2: *Applying Your Post-Its*

THE BACKWARD CLASSROOM

If you have a teacher who is frequently late to class, The Backward Classroom is a great trick. This prank must be pulled off with a partner who is willing to stand lookout.

How to Pull off The Backward Classroom:

You will need:	
• Desks • A partner	• Extreme pranking skills
Money required:	**Time required:**
Free	One day to plan, 30 minutes to execute
Success rate: 15 percent	**Mischief level:** 7

1. Before anyone gets to class, write a message on the blackboard. Try to make it look believable. The message should read:

> Dear Class,
> Please turn the room
> around backward.
>
> Signed, [YOUR TEACHER]

2 Leave the room. Have a partner stand lookout (see **How to Make a Lookout Station**, page 35).

3 Stroll in just before class begins. Most of your class should already be there. Pretend to notice the message. (You really need to **sell it** here.)

4 Convince classmates that the message is real by simply turning your desk and encouraging your classmates to obey the instructions. Get a friend to help you move the teacher's desk to the back of the room. Work quickly and calmly. It should look like the room has been flipped 180 degrees.

5 Signal your partner by cell phone when the switch is complete, so your partner can return to class.

Sell it: To convince others that a hoax is real.

ADDITIONAL MISCHIEF IDEAS:

- Rotate the room ninety degrees, so everyone's facing the window. (Better view.)
- Rotate the room by just a *few degrees*, so the teacher knows *something's* wrong, but can't figure out quite what.
- Write PLEASE MEET ME IN THE GYM, WHERE TODAY'S CLASS WILL BE HELD. Then convince everyone to go to the gym.

✓ On a piece of paper, write the names of each of your teachers. Over the next ten days, count which teachers are late, and how many times. Then take this number, multiply it by ten, and subtract that number from one hundred. This gives you that teacher's **On-Time Percentage (OTP)**.

For instance, if Ms. Jenkins is late two out of every ten days, her OTP is eighty percent $(100 - (2 \times 10))$. You want teachers with low OTPs. The best OTP would be zero percent— they're just late every day.

The OTP is an extremely helpful tool in the prankster's arsenal.

THE ROAMING GNOME

If you're unfortunate enough to live in a neighborhood infested with a *garden gnome*, there's only one thing you can do: Return it to the wild.

Garden gnomes are horrid creatures that some people keep in their yard to ward off evil. They can be identified by their pointy red hats, long white beards, and occasionally a pipe.

FIGURE 1: THE GARDEN GNOME

The prank begins when the owner of the gnome receives a letter in the mail:

> I've gone off to
> travel the world.
>
> SIGNED, YOUR GNOME

You can get creative with the letter. Give the gnome a name. Make up an elaborate story for why he's leaving. Say he got tired of sitting in the garden. Complain that the bushes wouldn't shut up. Gnomes should be feisty.

Over the next few weeks, the gnome owner should receive a series of photos or postcards from exotic locations like Egypt and New Jersey, with the gnome pictured in each photo. After this "trip" around the world, the owner comes out to the garden one morning to find that the gnome has silently returned.

The best time to stage this prank is just before you're about to go on a long vacation. You put the gnome in your luggage, then get pictures of the creature as you travel around the world. The modern twist is to take digital photos, and send them back to the owner via online postcards, but for this you'll need to know the gnome owner's e-mail address.

The difficulty with this prank is that most people do not live in gnome-infested neighborhoods. (Most gnomes live deep underground, guarding buried treasure and eating yak.) Also, many lawn gnomes are too heavy to lift, and would be impossible to carry to China in your luggage.

The Traveling Gnome works better for small indoor gnomes, or any strange objects that might be capable of walking away: desk toys, dolls, mascots, or statues. Be careful not to take anything too heavy, too breakable, or too expensive. And if you break it, you must buy it.

If you're not planning a vacation anytime soon, and

you're handy with graphics editing programs like Photoshop, you can take a digital picture of the gnome, and paste in backgrounds of exotic locations, like Cairo and Hoboken. Then send e-mails to the gnome owner, each one telling about an increasingly crazy adventure.

A nice final touch is to bring back a "souvenir" of the gnome's travels: a picture of the Great Pyramids, or something from the mall in New Jersey. Leave it with the gnome when you return it. This can also be a nice thank-you gift to the gnome's owner for letting you borrow their gnome for several weeks.

TECHNOLOGY TOMFOOLERY

THREE EASY COMPUTER PRANKS

1. **Change their home page.** Open the web browser they normally use, and change the home page to something silly or annoying (look under the Options or Settings menu for home page options). The most annoying page in the world, by the way, can be found at: www.mischiefmakersmanual.com/tools/annoy.

2. **Change AutoCorrect.** Microsoft Word has a feature called AutoCorrect that will look for misspelled words and automatically correct them for you. You can set this to look for *any word*, and replace it with *any other word*. Try changing their name to the name of an animal, like "platypus" or "ocelot." Take a common word like "the" and replace it with a funny word like "nut" or "pants."

3. **Send an EEEEE! Card.** Find a site that offers free e-cards (www.hallmark.com, for example) and customize them with your own mischievous messages like, "I LIKE HAM!" or "I'm sorry I ran over your cat." Best of all, Hallmark e-mails the EEEEE! Card for you!

THREE EASY CELL PHONE PRANKS

1. **Change their ringtone.** This one's so easy that an adult can do it. Most phones have a variety of funny or weird ringtones built in: wacky disco beats, clucking chickens, etc. When they're not looking, change their ringtone, and set the volume as loud as it will go.

2. **Change their default message.** Most cell phones have a little text greeting that you can customize (usually through the Settings or Options menu). Change it to read something different, like "NO SERVICE" or "I LIKE CHEESEBURGERS!"

3 | **Change their numbers.** In the cell phone contact list, look for frequently dialed numbers ("HOME," "CHURCH," "MOM," etc.), then replace them with *prank* numbers (local pizza shop, a different church, the White House, etc.).

THREE EASY INSTANT MESSENGER PRANKS

1 | **Change their away message.** Many people set up "away messages" to auto-respond to instant messages while they're away from the computer. Change this to read something like, "I DON'T SHOWER VERY OFTEN" or "CAN'T COME TO THE COMPUTER RIGHT NOW, EATING A TWELVE-POUND MEATBALL."

2 | **Reach out and prank someone.** Get access to their computer, then start messaging random people in their contact list. Make bizarre requests and outlandish claims. No one will know it's you. (This works even better with text messaging on someone else's cell phone.)

3 | **Change their screen name.** Okay, this one's not quite so easy, but it's awesome. Find out which IM network they belong to, then register for a new account. Give this account a ridiculous name, like "monkeybutt232." *Export* their contact list from their old IM account (usually under Options), then *import* them into the new account. Set their IM program to sign in automatically, so they never notice the difference—until people start replying, "Monkeybutt232? WHO IS THIS?!" You've changed their identity!

☑ Try any **three** of the above pranks (Computer, Cell
Phone, or Instant Messenger Pranks), or invent a
new one of your choosing.

PRANK #1: _____

NOTES: _____

_____

PRANK #2: _____

NOTES: _____

_____

PRANK #3: _____

NOTES: _____

_____

PUBLICIZING YOUR PRANKS

KEEPING YOUR COVER

Most of the time you should conduct your mischief quietly, never drawing attention to yourself. There's no reason to take credit for your pranks. It just makes you look suspicious, and gets you in trouble. Give yourself a fake name, like "Banana Bandito" or "The Dark Five," and let your alternate personality get all the attention.

As you move into more ambitious mischief, however, you will sometimes want to get your prank noticed by a wider audience, like when you're trying to create a **hoax** (page 216). The good news is, from **Blogging** to **Getting on the News** (page 212), it's easier than ever to become famous.

BLOGGING

People, in general, trust what they read. Even on the Internet, where you should never trust *anything*, people read **blogs** and say, "Well, it's probably true. I read it on a blog."

Blogs can be very useful for getting yourself noticed—not just in your city or town, but the *entire world*. And they're easier than ever to set up, and *completely free* (see next page)!

TOP FOUR FREE BLOGGING SERVICES

1. www.blogger.com
2. www.wordpress.com
3. www.livejournal.com
4. www.typepad.com

Let's say you want to create the rumor that a particular local coffee shop in your town is closing down to make room for a Laundromat. You might start a blog about the coffee shop a few months beforehand. You should make it look real. You should post to your blog every few days with news about the coffee shop, which you can just rewrite from somewhere else.

Wisconsin coffee shop makes way for Laundromat!

The trick to creating a believable blog hoax is to build up a history of posting on the blog. You can't have only one entry, or people will figure out immediately that it's a prank. You have to put some time into it, which will really pay off in the end. Besides, blogging is fun.

Don't get fancy. Keep your design simple; loud, flashy colors are a dead giveaway. Be careful with spelling and grammar. Get yourself a unique domain name if possible.

Once you've posted your hoax post, you need to get it noticed. You're about to learn how.

WIKIPEDIA

The online encyclopedia known as **Wikipedia** is possibly the least reliable reference source in the world, because *anyone can edit it.* Really. Anyone. At any time. From any computer.

Wikipedia operates under the idea that "people are generally good." (There are exceptions.) When you see something that's incorrect, or that contains a spelling error, you can go into **edit mode** by clicking the "edit this page" tab at the top of the page.

Certain articles get "locked down" if many people try to change them randomly (these are usually articles about famous people, like the president). Stay away from those articles. The other *nine million articles* are yours for the taking.

For instance, let's say you want to convince someone that

the all-time Guitar Hero high score is held by a monkey. You can easily go into the "Guitar Hero" entry in Wikipedia and type, "The all-time high score for Guitar Hero is held by a monkey with twelve toes. Her name is Sheila, and she wears panties on her head."

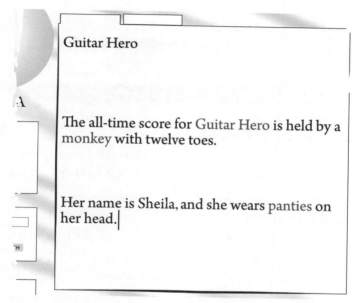

As soon as you click "Save Page," that's what everyone will see, *every time* they read the article!

On popular articles, this will get noticed and fixed very quickly, so it's best to pick obscure topics or historical figures for your Wikipedia pranks. Just find a way to link the topic back to your prank.

Now you see how easy it is to get yourself, or your prank,

mentioned on Wikipedia. It's huge. It's your fifteen minutes of fame. If you're lucky, you could even get your prank referenced in *print*, because some adults now use Wikipedia as a reference source, *in books!**

> ☑ Research a topic on Wikipedia. Click "Edit this page," and make a harmless edit to the page (changing punctuation or rewording a sentence).
>
> WWW.MISCHIEFMAKERSMANUAL.COM

GETTING ON THE NEWS

Getting on the news is easier than ever. There are so many different *kinds* of news (see **Kinds of News**), and all of them need **stories**. Your prank, if it's ambitious or funny enough, will be a great story. The people who collect these stories are sometimes called "journalists," and they can get your prank seen by thousands, if not millions, of people.

When you've pulled off a particularly excellent prank, the most important thing is to get *photo proof.* Take a few pictures, or shoot some video. Then write up a *short description* of your prank (one to two paragraphs if possible). A good photo plus a good description is what reporters call "a good story." A great photo plus a great description is what reporters call "a great story." Try to make yours a great story.

Most reporters love funny stories about people doing wacky things. The trick is to find the *right* reporter. Don't

---

* See en.wikipedia.org/wiki/Wikipedia

send in a general e-mail through a website or a "letter to the editor." This never works. Instead, look for the names of the three top people in the right department.

FOR THIS TYPE OF NEWS	LOOK FOR THIS PERSON	HERE'S WHERE TO LOOK
TV	• Producer • Supervising producer • Coordinating producer	TV station's website
Newspapers	Some kind of "Editor" (but not Editor In Chief)	The **masthead**, which is the page where they list all the names, usually in section A
Blogs	The blogger	"Contact Us" link
Radio	• Radio producer • Production director	Listen for a call-in number; check station's website

The easiest place to get noticed is **blogs**. Find a couple of bloggers who like funny stuff and send them your story. Getting publicity is like fishing: Sometimes they bite, and sometimes they don't. Keep trying. When you get a bite, it's worth the wait.

Another good place to start is **morning radio shows**,

especially rock stations. They love anything having to do with pranks or practical jokes, and they'll report pretty much anything you tell them. E-mail them your story through the website, an hour before the show begins.

The nice thing about **newspapers** is that every town has one, and most small towns are kind of slow in the news department. Local newspaper reporters especially love anything that happens at a huge, identifiable town landmark.

That's a trick that also works with **local television**. But try not to make your prank too "regional." If it's a prank that's funny to people in other towns, then your story will often get rebroadcast on other news stations. If you're extremely lucky, it'll be a slow news day, and CNN will need a quick little story to fill time before a commercial. Before you know it, your prank has just made national news.

This kind of thing happens all the time. It can happen to you. Just be creative and persistent. Don't give up easily.

✓ Identify five sources of local news for your town (newspaper, radio, TV, or Internet).

NEWS SOURCE #1: _____

NEWS SOURCE #2: _____

NEWS SOURCE #3: _____

NEWS SOURCE #4: _____

NEWS SOURCE #5: _____

KINDS OF NEWS

CNN News
NBC News
ABC News
CBS News
BBC News
PBS News
CNBC News
FOX News
MTV News
Telemundo News
Local TV news
Cable access news
Geraldo Rivera specials
Satellite radio stations
FM radio stations
AM radio stations
Podcasts
New York Times
Wall Street Journal
USA Today
National Enquirer
Weekly World News
City newspaper
Town newspaper
School newspaper
GRIT
Flyers handed out an event

HOW TO HOAX

GREAT HOAXERS OF HISTORY

A **hoax** is the highest form of prank, practiced only by the very best mischief makers in history. To pull off a hoax, you must get a large number of people to believe a fake story, like a **Fake Historical Artifact** (page 226) or a **Fake Alien Landing** (page 232). To learn how to hoax properly, you must first study the masters.

1. **William Horace de Vere Cole** (1881–1936). A master of dressing up like important people (politicians, the Sultan of Zanzibar, etc.) and getting people to believe he was actually that person. Got all kinds of fancy tours and dinners just by wearing the right **costume** (page 41).

2. **George Hull** (1829–1888). Created the famous "Cardiff Giant," a 10-foot-tall "petrified man" that he buried underground, then pretended to discover a year later. Charged admission for people to look at it, and made a small fortune until someone figured it out (but by then, he had sold it).

3. **Alan Abel** (1930–). Tricked news programs like the *Today Show* into believing ridiculous stories, like a violin quartet that plays topless. Once tricked the *New York Times* into running a death notice for him, even though he was alive and well!

Write a short summary of a famous hoax that occurred at some point in history. Google "famous hoaxes" for research ideas. Use at least two sources for your report.

NOTES: _____

_____

_____

_____

_____

_____

_____

_____

_____

_____

_____

_____

_____

_____

_____

_____

_____

_____

_____

ABOMINABLE SNOWMAN FOOTPRINTS

No mischief maker's education is complete without learning about **Hugh Troy** (1906–1964), an American painter who was known for a lifetime of clever and hilarious pranks. When you become a Master Mischief Maker, people begin creating myths about *you*. You become a legend. Hugh Troy was a legend.

One of the "legends of Troy" was a prank that he *may have* pulled on a famous art teacher, Louis Agassiz Fuertes, while Troy was his student at Cornell University. Fuertes was a famous painter of birds, and had traveled the world many times, collecting various animal parts over the years: bones, skeletons, etc.

Troy borrowed a couple of rhinoceros feet, then attached them to the bottom of two pails. Then he threaded a long rod through the pail handles, and with a friend, used the contraption to make a series of "rhinoceros tracks" in the snow, leading down to a nearby lake. Troy then cut a huge scraggly hole in the ice, to make it look as if the great beast had lumbered onto the ice, then dropped in.

Since the school's drinking water came from the lake, many students quit drinking the "rhino-fied" water until Troy sent in an anonymous letter explaining how he did the stunt.

Here's how to make a modern version of the "Hugh Troy Rhino-Tracker," using parts available from your local Home Depot or hardware store.

How to Make Abominable Snowman Footprints:

You will need:	
• A long, sturdy metal rod or piece of wood (an adjustable shower rod works well)	• 2" thick Styrofoam (available at craft stores like Jo-Ann Fabrics)
• Two buckets with handles	• Piece of paper
• Duct tape	• Marker
	• Scissors
	• Handsaw

Money required:	Time required:	
Less than $30.00	2-3 hours	
Success rate: 65 percent	**Mischief level:** 7	

1. Draw your footprint design on a piece of paper. Cut it out.
2. Lay your paper stencil on the Styrofoam and trace the outline.
3. Using the saw, cut the abominable "footprint" out of Styrofoam.

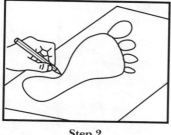
Step 2

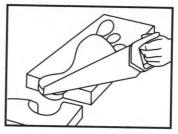
Step 3

4. Repeat for the other foot.
5. Using duct tape, secure the Styrofoam footprints to the

bottom of the pails. Wrap around the sides only, not the bottom. Be sure the handle of the pail is pointing to the *top and bottom* of the footprint, not the sides.

6 Now put your rod or pole through the bucket handles. Hold it steady, and have a partner duct tape the handles to the rod, so they don't slip.

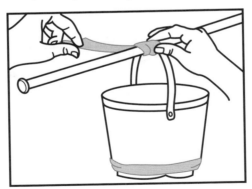

7 Find something heavy to put in each bucket (as heavy as the two of you can comfortably lift).

8 Walk your contraption outside, and put in the weights. Practice making footprints with your partner, each of you holding one end of the pole.

9 Once you're good at tracking, walk the contraption to a place with unbroken snow, and lay your handiwork.

10 Be sure to take pictures. Send them into *Weekly World News*.

This is a brilliant prank for its simplicity (easy to build) and versatility (easy to change):

- It can be improvised from any number of parts (branches, string, rubber bands, etc.).
- It can be set up in a wide variety of winter locations (school playgrounds, Starbucks parking lots, etc.).
- You can also adapt the prank for use in the mud or sand (perfect for freaking out people at camps and campgrounds).

✓ Modify the design on the previous page so that
it can be used for **Dinosaur Tracks in the Snow**,
complete with a swishing of the dinosaur's massive
tail.

YOUR SOLUTION: _____

_____

_____

_____

_____

_____

_____

_____

_____

_____

_____

_____

_____

_____

_____

_____

_____

_____

_____

_____

_____

_____

FAKE HISTORICAL ARTIFACTS

The **Piltdown Man** is a famous hoax that originated in 1912, when the archaeologist Charles Dawson supposedly uncovered the skull and jawbone of a "prehistoric man" that was unlike anything discovered up to that point. Dawson speculated that this caveman represented a "missing link" in the evolution of ape to man. He named it *Eoanthropus dawsoni* (Latin for "Dawson's dawn-man"). *He named it after himself.*

And it was all a prank.

From the beginning, people were suspicious. But somehow most scientists believed it, if you can believe this, for *forty years.* This has to be considered the Greatest Hoax of All Time, because it took that long for the scientific community to figure out that it was an old human skull and some orangutan teeth, stained in dye and buried in dirt for a while. *Orangutan teeth!*

At least 38 of Charles Dawson's archeological "discoveries" were later found to be fakes, including ancient stone tools, boats, and a sea serpent. But the Piltdown Man was Dawson's masterpiece: It changed the course of history, confusing scientists for decades about the true timeline of human evolution.

Most adults aren't so good at history, so they won't remember the Piltdown Man. That's good for you, because it gives you the chance to create a similar "fossil prank" for only a few dollars. It's perfect for getting extra credit in history class, or just to see if your science teacher is paying attention.

How to Make a Fake Historical Artifact:

You will need:

- Paper
- Newspaper
- Cardboard
- Masking tape
- Paper towels
- Crayola Model Magic Fusion (available at Wal-Mart or Target)
- Small skewer or toothpick
- Ziploc bag
- Dirt

Money required:	Time required:
Less than $20.00	Several days

Success rate:	55 percent	Mischief level:	7

1. Fossils should be big. The easiest parts to fake are the tooth and the claw. For this example, we'll fake a tooth from the **megalodon**, an enormous prehistoric shark.

2. Learn as much as possible about your fake, so it will be easier to talk about the subject with confidence. The megalodon, which died out millions of years ago, is thought to be the largest flesh-eating fish in recorded history, so its teeth are *enormous*. They look like massive shark teeth, perfect for shredding helpless whales.

3. Draw a picture of the tooth on paper. It should be about ten inches on its longest edge. Don't use straight lines or right angles, since they will make the tooth look like a fake. Make it slightly imperfect.

4. When the shape looks like the picture, cut it out with

scissors. Using this paper as a stencil, trace the shape onto a piece of cardboard.

5　Make the cardboard tooth thicker by attaching small wads of newspaper. Take a quarter sheet, crumple a corner into a wad, and fold the rest of the paper over your wad, creating a fat packet of paper, about the size of a large oatmeal cookie.

6　Wrap your wad with a few strands of masking tape, then attach it to the tooth with more masking tape. Keep the masking tape as smooth as possible. Use plenty of masking tape; the tooth should be almost as much masking tape as newspaper.

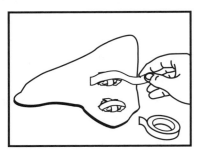

7 Make more paper cookies and add them to the cardboard tooth, building up the thickness. Try to define two parts of the tooth, the "root" and the "blade," by making the root more thick and bumpy.

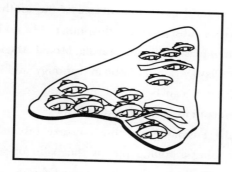

8 Use more masking tape down the blade, to smooth out rough spots. Try to make the blade slightly curved, and as smooth as possible. Apply lots of pieces of masking tape to the blade of the tooth, from the root toward the tip.

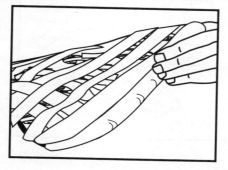

9 If you have low spots, you can crumple up a bit of paper, push it into the void, and tape it down flat. But don't worry if it has problems. Of course it's chipped and flawed! *It's been buried in a rock for fifteen million years!* As long as it's pointy, it'll look like a tooth.

10 When you run out of masking tape, you are done. Next you must cover the surface of the tooth. You can use various substances for this, but the best choice is a modeling plastic called **Crayola Model Magic Fusion**. It's like Play-Doh, but plastic and spongy, and it hardens as it dries. It can be found at Target, Toys "R" Us, or Amazon.com for about ten dollars.

11 Press the Fusion into a thin pancake (about 1/8 inch thick), using a rolling pin or the palm of your hand. Cover the entire tooth with a layer of the pressed Fusion pancake. Apply it in pieces, blending all the seams into one another, so that the skin is complete. (To smooth seams, lay a paper towel on the surface, and rub it lightly.)

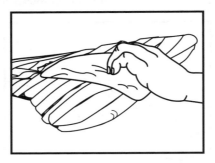

12 Keep the surface rough, especially around the root. Make it look ancient by poking small "pockmarks" on the root, using a skewer or round toothpick. Add some ridges to the blade by lightly dragging a toothpick down the surface.

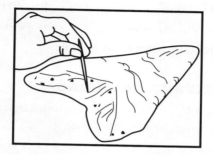

13 The blade, on the other hand, should look smooth and enamel. Wet a paper towel and gently polish the surface.

14 Sit back and admire your masterpiece. Then hide it in a closet. Model Magic Fusion dries in seventy-two hours.

15 When your prank tooth has fossilized, put it in a bucket of wet dirt, then wipe away the excess.

16 Depending on your story, you can either let the dirt dry for a few days, or keep it wet (for a "freshly discovered" look). Either way, you should put the tooth in a Ziploc bag or other display case—somewhere people can look at it, but not too closely. Under no circumstances should anyone be allowed to take out or touch the fossil. Explain that it is too valuable and delicate.

17 [Optional] Create a fake "Certificate of Authenticity" from a country like China. Detail the date and location of the discovery.

Before presenting your fossil, make sure you have your story straight. Perhaps you received the tooth from a relative who traveled to China, or maybe you bought it off the Internet. Just whatever you do, don't name it "The Piltdown Tooth." People are gullible, but not *that* gullible.

HOW TO FAKE AN ALIEN LANDING

In the late 1970s, farmers throughout England began to notice a very strange thing: giant circles that were forming, overnight, in their fields. Someone, or *something*, was flattening down the crops, in *perfect geometric patterns.*

People came up with all kinds of explanations about what caused the mysterious circles in these farmers' crops. In the 1980s, the media began to broadcast the story of these "crop circles," which led to even more sightings, and more theories.

Some people claimed crop circles were evidence of UFOs. It was possible, after all, that the circles could have been made by an enormous spaceship with a perfectly smooth bottom, which landed silently, then took off again without any further damage to the field.

Or it could have been a bunch of guys with boards and rope.

Doug Bower and Dave Chorley were two English pranksters who wanted to fool people into thinking UFOs had landed, so they began creating crop circles at night, using the method revealed on the next page.

Although not all crop circles can be attributed to these types of pranksters, experts say almost eighty percent are clearly man-made. And what about the other twenty percent? Either aliens, or better pranksters.

The instructions below explain how to make a crop circle in a large field, but large backyards are also good targets, especially if you can view the yard from a high window and the grass hasn't been mowed in a while. It's actually a good way to get out of mowing the lawn, since no one will want to disturb it.

How to Fake an Alien Landing:

You will need:	
• One large flat plank, about six inches wide, and between four and six feet long • Rope • String	• A skinny pole or stake (tent stake will do) • Hammer • Several flashlights (a headlamp is excellent) • Sturdy hiking boots or shoes
Money required:	**Time required:**
Less than $20.00	Several hours
Success rate: 40 percent	**Mischief level:** 9

1 Select your field. Make sure it is easily visible from above, preferably next to a high road or other viewing area that gets a lot of visitors. By daylight, figure out where you're going to make your pattern. You can also measure the field and use graph paper to plot your pattern.

2 Drill two large holes in the plank, one at either end. Cut a length of rope that's a foot or two longer than

the board, and tie it through each hole, securing with a knot. This is what crop circle prankster John Lundberg calls the "stalk stomper."

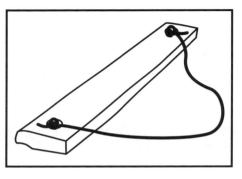

3 At night, sneak to the field with your supplies. Walk into the field at the center point of your circle, trying not to leave any footprints behind you. Using your hammer, pound in the stake. This will be the center point of your circle.

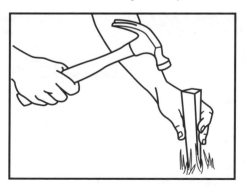

4 Cut a length of string. The circle will be about double the length of this string.

5 Tie the string to the stake. Tie the other end to the rope.

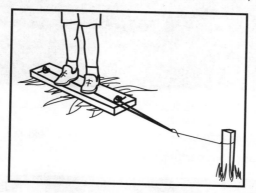

6 Walk out until the string is taut, and make sure the board is pointing to the stake. Stamp down on the plank, pressing all the stalks in one direction until they are flat.

7 Lift the board, take a step, and repeat, making sure all the stalks are flattened. When you have completed the edge of the circle, go back toward the stake and finish flattening the inside stalks.

8 When the circle is complete, dig up your stake, fill in the hole, and leave as quietly as you came, trying not to leave any footprints.

9 Be sure to call local reporters the next morning, and leave an anonymous suggestion that they check out the field.

When trying to figure out whether something is real or a hoax, it often helps to remember **Occam's Razor**. In other words, when faced with the explanation that it's *either* UFOs *or* boards and rope, it's probably boards and rope.

OCCAM'S RAZOR

Not a shaving instrument, but an idea that when trying to explain something complicated (like circles in a field), *the simplest solution is usually the right solution.* UFOs are a complicated solution; boards and rope are an easy solution. Occam's Razor is not always right, but it's useful as a guide.

☑ Memorize Occam's Razor. Be able to explain the idea to a partner.

WWW.MISCHIEFMAKERSMANUAL.COM

MASSIVE MISCHIEF

SMOKE BOMBS

Every young mischief maker wants to know how to make smoke bombs. The trick is how to do it *safely*. There are lots of dangerous smoke bomb recipes out there. The beautiful thing about *this* smoke bomb recipe is that it's safe, as long as you follow the rules of **Proper Smoke Bomb Etiquette** (see page 239).

This smoke bomb shoots a beautiful stream of jet smoke out the top of a ping-pong ball. And the only ingredients you need are ping-pong balls, aluminum foil, and tape—items you can safely pick up at Wal-Mart. You can also build a larger version by simply cutting up more ping-pong balls and piling them in a larger square of aluminum foil.

This is a good use for old dented ping-pong balls, by the way. Don't use your family's good ping-pong balls, because then you can't play ping-pong.

How to Make a . . . Well, *You Know*:

You will need:	
• 4-6 ping-pong balls • Electrical tape	• Scissors • A straw (optional)
Money required:	**Time required:**
Less than $20.00	Several hours

Success rate:	75 percent	**Mischief level:**	8

1 Poke a hole in the top of a ping-pong ball using a sharp pick, or the tip of your scissors. **Be careful that you do not cut yourself with the scissors.** The hole should be large enough to fit a straw.

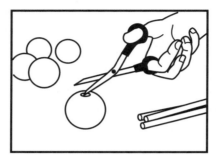

2 Cut the rest of the ping-pong balls into small pieces (small enough to fit in the hole).

3 Put each of the pieces into the ping-pong ball.

4 Cut a one-inch piece of straw and put it into the ping-pong ball, so it is poking out the top. Tape it in place.

5 Wrap the entire ball in aluminum foil, up to the top of the straw. Make sure the entire ball is wrapped.

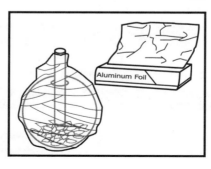

6 Light the ball from the bottom. Once the foil has ignited, RUN!

PROPER SMOKE BOMB ETIQUETTE

1. *Keep away from people.* Ignite them in a distant parking lot or an abandoned building. People get panicky when they see smoke, and someone always gets in trouble. Make sure they don't see it.
2. *Keep away from anything flammable.* Smoke bombs involve fire, so do not light them near anything flammable. (Stay away from garages.) Be careful of dry grass. Pavement and gravel make ideal surfaces.
3. *Keep away once lit.* Use a kitchen lighter or a long match to light the smoke bomb. And once the foil has ignited, get away.

THE SCIENCE OF SMOKE

The flammable ingredient in ping-pong balls is **celluloid** (otherwise known as cellulose nitrate), the very first plastic, invented in the late 1860s. When exposed to fire and air, celluloid will *melt, smoke,* and then *burst into flame.* (Bet you never knew ping-pong balls were so dangerous.)

Learn these facts. That way, if you're caught, you can tell someone you're "performing a scientific experiment on the flammability of celluloid," and you'll be telling the truth. People are usually afraid to mess with experiments.

SUDS MOUNTAIN

As you near the completion of your training, young prankster, you should know about the mysterious substance known as **dry ice**. It can be used to make toilets and urinals ooze a creepy, Halloween-like smoke. It can be used to turn a swimming pool into a creepy witches' brew. And it can be used to create a *small mountain of foamy suds.*

Dry ice is frozen carbon dioxide, and it's extremely cold (110 degrees below zero). **Never touch it with your bare hands**. Always wear gloves or mittens—*dry ice is so cold that it can burn.* You should store dry ice in a cooler or ice chest, and use it the same day you buy it. Don't keep it in the freezer, as it is so cold it can shut down some thermostats!

Because it's so cold, dry ice is used to pack groceries or frozen goods, so you can often get it at your local grocery store or ice-cream store for around a dollar per pound. It's easier to find around Halloween. Make some phone calls. If they ask why, tell them you're having a party.

ICE ICE BABY

The reason it's called "dry" ice is because it doesn't melt into water, like regular "wet" ice—it goes directly from a frozen solid into a *gas*. Which gas? *Carbon dioxide.*

How to Make Suds Mountain:

You will need:	
• Dry ice • Water (the hotter, the better) • Bucket or pail • Bubble solution (get it at the toy store)	• Glycerin (get it at the drugstore or grocery store, in the baking aisle)

Money required:	Time required:
Less than $30.00	Several days

Success rate:	85 percent	Mischief level:	8

1. Carry the ingredients outside to their final location.

2. Dump the hot water, the bubble solution, and the glycerin into the bucket. The best recipe is to use equal parts water, bubbles, and glycerin, but do the best with what you have. You can also add a squirt of food coloring for the creep effect.

3. Drop the dry ice into the bucket, and stand back!

This also makes a hilarious yet harmless Halloween prank—just pour the bubble solution into a jack-o'-lantern, drop in the dry ice, put the lid on, and run. Suds and bubbles will pour from the eyes and mouth, like a pumpkin with terrible allergies.

If you have any dry ice left over, you can also drop it in apple juice to make a tasty bubbly cider.

☑ Locate your nearest supplier of dry ice by calling local supermarkets and ice-cream shops. You never know when you're going to need it.

My nearest supplier is: _____

_____

Phone number: _____

WWW.MISCHIEFMAKERSMANUAL.COM

THE SUPEREST SOAKER

Forget wimpy water guns. Forget those huge plastic "water blasters." This is the most *powerful*, high-pressure homemade water cannon that you can build. Unleash a blast of water from one of these babies, and you will feel the fury of the gods. H_2 OH NOOOOOO!

The Superest Soaker requires the use of an **air compressor**, which is a heavy piece of machinery that can sometimes be found in garages or shop classes. Carpenters usually have one. You can also rent them (Google "tool rental" and your zip code), but they're very heavy to move without a car!

CAN'T HANDLE THE PRESSURE

This is not the kind of water gun that you point at people. This is the kind of water cannon that removes paint from the side of houses. Use common sense, and aim away from living things (with the possible exception of large trees).

How to Make The Superest Soaker:

You will need:

- Disposable fire extinguisher with a plastic head that you can screw on and off (check Wal-Mart or the hardware store)

- Air compressor
- Electrical tape
- Scissors
- Water

Money required:	Time required:
Less than $30.00	One day

Success rate:	60 percent	Mischief level:	9

1. Empty the fire extinguisher by spraying it into a tightly sealed trash bag. **Do not breathe the powder**, which can be harmful to the lungs and eyes.

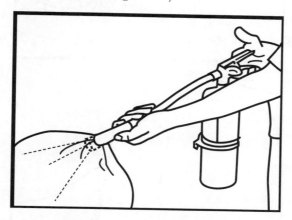

2. Unscrew the top to the fire extinguisher and rinse it thoroughly. This should be done in a utility sink in the

basement, or outside using a garden hose. Be sure to rinse out the tube and nozzle as well.

3 Cut off half of the white nozzle. Cover the remaining white part, plus the black part, with electrical tape. This is the nozzle for your water cannon.

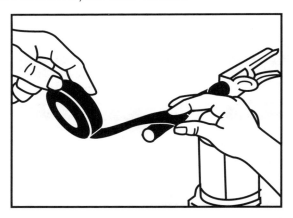

4 Fill the tank about 2/3 full with water. Screw on the cap.

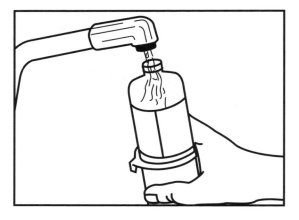

5 Set up the air compressor, and pressurize it to 105 PSI. **Do not set the air compressor higher than 105 PSI.** Make sure the valve to the compressor is turned off, so the compressor can build up pressure.

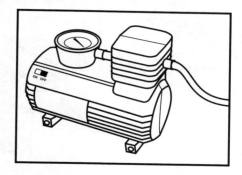

6 Put the compressor nozzle into the fire extinguisher nozzle. Hold it there firmly with your writing hand, pressing down on the fire extinguisher lever with your forearm. With your other hand, turn on the valve to the compressor. Watch the pressure gauge on the fire extinguisher; when it stops moving, you've reached 105 PSI.

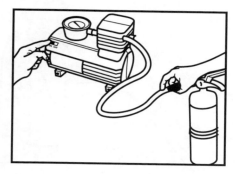

7 Remove your forearm from the fire extinguisher lever, then turn the valve to the compressor off. Remove the air compressor hose from the fire extinguisher.

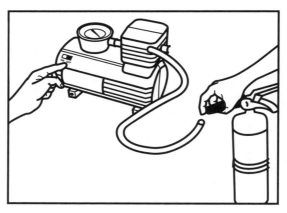

8 Shout "READY! AIM! *FIRE EXTINGUISHER!*" as you blast forth a *mighty jet spray from the blowhole of a whale.* Happy drenching!

☑ Design your own "Final Prank." This is a massive mischief mission that could be pulled on a famous local person, statue, or business. Using the Prankster's Code and all that you have learned to this point, outline the prank from start to finish. Be as detailed as possible.

_____
_____
_____
_____
_____
_____
_____
_____
_____
_____
_____
_____
_____
_____
_____
_____
_____
_____
_____

_____
_____
_____
_____
_____
_____
_____
_____
_____
_____
_____
_____
_____
_____
_____
_____
_____
_____
_____
_____

When you are finished with your design, write it
here, but do not pull off the prank. A good
prankster is disciplined, and can wait.

PRANK RANK ACHIEVED!

You have much to be proud of, young mischief maker. You have worked your way through yet another level of *M3*, which means you have now earned the title of **Massive Mischief Maker**. You are only one level away from reaching the greatest achievement of your young life: the rare and brilliant ranking of **Master Mischief Maker**. Graduation is within your grasp, grasshopper.

☑ Visit www.mischiefmakersmanual.com to track progress and download badge.

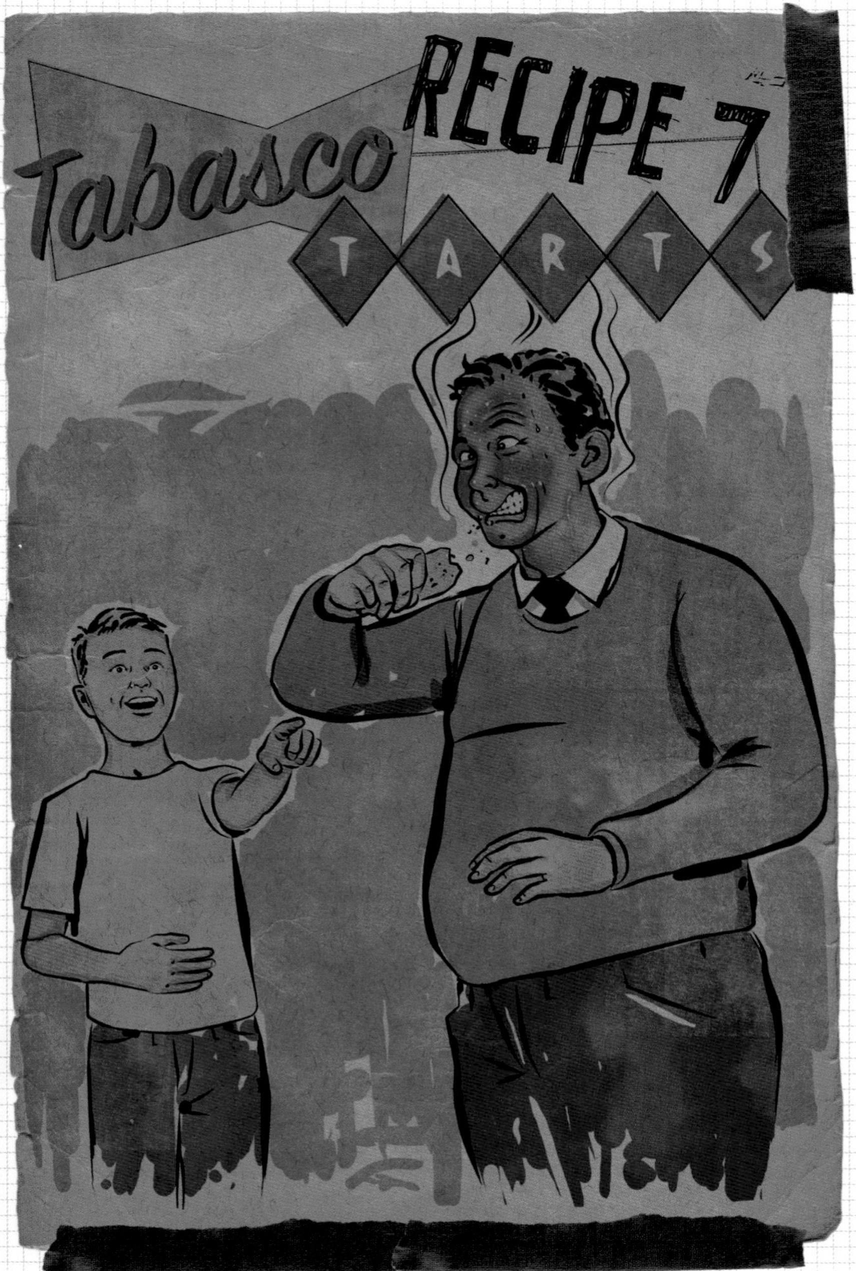
Tabasco
RECIPE 7
TARTS

If you don't complete this final section, you're going to get in trouble.

TROUBLE

CONFESSION

If you faithfully follow the instructions in *Mischief Maker's Manual*, your odds of getting in trouble will be *far lower* than those of untrained hooligans. Still, mischief happens. Despite your best planning, sometimes your principal catches you walking a live cow up the steps of your school. In case of emergency, here's what you should do.

1. **Remain calm.** This is an excellent skill to develop. People who are able to remain calm in dangerous situations are much better equipped to deal with life. Remaining calm will give you the upper hand in almost every situation. Your captor is likely to be frustrated or furious, which gives you the advantage. Breathe deeply, as you calmly analyze your situation.

2. **Remain silent.** Try to keep quiet. "You have the right to remain silent." Police are supposed to say this to criminals when they make an arrest, because most criminals are dumb, and try to talk their way out of it. It's smarter to keep your yapper shut. (Using the phrase "I would like to take the fifth" can sometimes impress a social studies teacher enough to let you go.) Keep quiet for as long as possible; sometimes this is hours, and sometimes this is less than a minute.

3. **Take responsibility.** Some adults are not stupid. They will see you are stalling for time, and threaten you with

punishment. Up to this point, they might still let you go, but once they start talking about punishment, they're serious. If they continue to threaten, you will have no choice but to confess.

TAKING THE FIFTH

This phrase refers to the Fifth Amendment in the Bill of Rights, which is the right to remain silent when being put on trial. Also known as "pleading the fifth," it basically means *not saying anything*, as anything you would say would dig yourself into a deeper hole.

TROUBLE

4 **Tell the truth.** When you confess, be absolutely truthful. At the same time, there is no reason to volunteer any more information than necessary. The urge to tell a lie is incredibly strong, but you must resist it. Besides, it's hard to keep track of lies. The truth is easy because it's, well, *the truth*.

5 **Apologize five times.** You should be absolutely, genuinely sorry, apologizing at least five times. You should say very little, except to say things like, "I know" and "You're right" and "I'm really very sorry." Don't get cute. Don't get sassy. Try to respond with "Yes, ma'am" and "No, sir." Be serious; don't joke. If possible, cry.

6 **Accept your defeat.** Your attitude will determine much of your punishment. Let your captors have their moment in the sun. They've won; you've lost. Accept that fact, and life will go much easier.

7 **Do not make any sudden moves.**

8 **Don't make excuses.** Take responsibility for your actions, for that is the mark of a professional mischief maker. By "owning up" to your actions, you will slowly regain the trust of adults, so that you can better fool them next time.

TROUBLE

WORST LIKELY SCENARIO

The ancient mischief masters had a saying: "Don't do the crime if you can't do the time."

That's a useful rule to remember throughout your mischief-making career. It means that before pulling off any prank, you should carefully think through the consequences of your actions. You shouldn't do the prank if you can't take the worst punishment you would be *likely* to receive.

The tricky part is that you must figure out the worst *likely* scenario, not the worst *possible* scenario. The best way to guess which punishment is *likely* is to study the *history* of punishment. What happened to other mischief makers who did similar things? Was their punishment consistent? Get a feel for who gives out the worst punishment, and try to avoid those people.

If you're unwilling to live with the worst likely punishment, then you shouldn't do it. End of story. Think up a new prank and move on. You must always be willing to live with the worst likely scenario, so make sure it is not expulsion from school, or excommunication from your family.

CRIME AND PUNISHMENT

Adults don't generally like to discipline kids. It's hard work, and often involves crying. It's not pleasant. This works in your favor.

When they do discipline, most adults lack imagination. In the olden days, mischief makers were subjected to spankings or canings (which can be thwarted by clenching your buttocks together tightly, or wearing bulky clothing under your pants).

Nowadays, most punishments fall into two basic categories:

1. **Making you do something.** This is usually something unpleasant, like cleaning dishes or scrubbing toilets. It may also be something academic, like an extra book report, or an essay on "The Role of the FDA, and Why They Had to Shut Down Our Cafeteria."

2. **Taking away something.** This can be your cell phone, computer, video game, TV, or online banking privileges. The only thing that really hurts about this is the loss of power. You can usually convince your parents to reduce the sentence after a few days. But why? Punishment is a great time to read a book, and work on your next great prank.

THE FIVE LEVELS OF TROUBLE

Trouble can be grouped into the following five categories. You should memorize these categories, so that if you're ever caught, you can calmly analyze your situation and the punishment likely to be given out. This will give you much more control over your situation.

Level 1: Slap on the Wrists. This kind of punishment hurts about as much as a slap on the wrists—just a quick sting, then it's over. A lecture or "talking to" is a popular slap-on-the-wrist punishment. This is the adult way of saying that what you did was not really that serious.

Level 2: Grounding. Longer punishments that involve losing some privilege (video game, going outside, eating, etc.), which only hurt because they represent the loss of your freedom. Accept your temporary loss, and you will feel much better for it. A **detention** is being grounded at school. Usually a detention involves sitting quietly in a room after school. Grounding isn't so bad; it gives you more time to think.

Level 3: Suspension. This comes in two forms: Out-of-School Suspension (sometimes abbreviated OSS) and In-School Suspension (sometimes abbreviated ISS). You usually have to complete extra work during your suspension, and you may not receive any credit for it. Usually parents are involved. You don't want to be here.

Level 4: Expulsion. This is where you are permanently removed from a school. The teachers and principal, literally, don't know what to do with you. You have driven your school to the brink of madness, and the only way to restore things to normal is to get rid of you entirely.

Level 5: Boarding School. Only after your parents have had as much as they can stand will they send you to a school far away, in hopes that someone there can straighten you out. In reality, this introduces you to a wide variety of new teachers and classmates to prank.

 Memorize the 8 steps of confession, the 2 types of punishment, and the 5 levels of trouble. Be able to explain each of these concepts to a trusted partner.

PRANK RANK ACHIEVED!

It has been a long journey, young prankster. You have read, memorized, cooked, built, and lit on fire. You have pranked hard. And you have learned well.

By completing all the exercises in this manual, you have earned the ultimate rank of **Master Mischief Maker**. You have become a *trained master* of mischief, kind of like a Jedi master, but much funnier. Well done, young locust. Well done.

☑ Visit www.mischiefmakersmanual.com to track progress and download badge.

As a Master Mischief Maker, or M3, you join the secret ranks of *an exclusive group* of pranksters worldwide. Though you may never know their names, you will recognize them by the quality of their mischief, by the daring and genius of their pranks. They come from cities and towns all over the world. There may even be some in your school!

Your M3 title is a reason to be proud. But always remember the title is nothing, unless you *live* that title every day. Mischief making is a lifelong endeavor. You must never lose your curiosity, your creativity, your sense of playfulness and fun. Pranksters give joy to the world. They make people laugh, and laughing is one of the most important things you can do. Especially when it's an *evil* laugh.

ABOUT M3

ABOUT M3 INSTITUTE

The **M3 Institute** researches and develops the world's most cutting-edge mischief, publishing its findings in the form of this training guide, *Sir John Hargrave's Mischief Maker's Manual.*

Using state-of-the-art pranking technology, the M3 Institute field-tests each of the gags in this manual for quality, safety, and reliability. It also develops wackier, more modern mischief in its high-tech **M3 Labs**.

The exact location of the Institute is classified.

ABOUT THE M3 STAFF

The staff at M3 Institute are some of the highest-ranked mischief makers in the world.

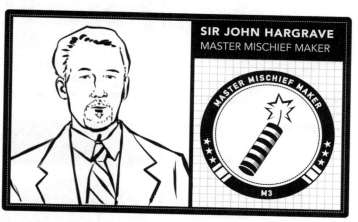

TED HAMMOND
MASSIVE MISCHIEF MAKER

DUSTY DEYO
MASSIVE MISCHIEF MAKER

For much more mischief, visit
www.mischiefmakersmanual.com.

M3 INSTITUTE HONORARY HEROES

Jade Hargrave	Bonnie Bader
Isaac Hargrave	Al Natanagara
Luke Rocket Hargrave	Lee Calderon
Cathy Hemming	Shelah DeJesus
Rob Valois	Meagan Bennett